Connecting Students
to STEM
Careers

Social Networking Strategies

Camille Cole

International Society for Technology in Education
EUGENE, OREGON • WASHINGTON, DC

Connecting Students to STEM Careers
Social Networking Strategies

Camille Cole

Director of Book Publishing: *Courtney Burkholder*
Acquisitions Editor: *Jeff V. Bolkan*
Production Editors: *Lynda Gansel, Tina Wells*
Production Coordinator: *Rachel Williams*
Graphic Designer: *Signe Landin*
Copy Editor: *Kristin Landon*
Proofreader: *Nancy Olson*
Indexer: *Pilar Wyman, Wyman Indexing*
Cover/Book Design and Production: *Kim McGovern*

Library of Congress Cataloging-in-Publication Data

Cole, Camille.
   Connecting students to STEM careers : social networking strategies / Camille Cole. — 1st ed.
     p. cm.
   Includes bibliographical references and index.
   ISBN 978-1-56484-291-6 (pbk.)
   1. Science—Study and teaching. 2. Technology—Study and teaching. 3. Science—Vocational guidance. 4. Technology—Vocational guidance. 5. Internet in education. 6. Online social networks.   I. Title.
   Q197.C65 2011
   507.1—dc23

                    2011023160

First Edition
ISBN: 978-1-56484-291-6
Printed in the United States of America

Cover Image: ©iStockphoto.com/Russell Tate
ISTE® is a registered trademark of the International Society for Technology in Education.

SUSTAINABLE FORESTRY INITIATIVE
Label applies to the text stock
Certified Fiber Sourcing
www.sfiprogram.org

About ISTE

The International Society for Technology in Education (ISTE) is the trusted source for professional development, knowledge generation, advocacy, and leadership for innovation. ISTE is the premier membership association for educators and education leaders engaged in improving teaching and learning by advancing the effective use of technology in PK–12 and teacher education.

Home of the National Educational Technology Standards (NETS) and ISTE's annual conference and exposition (formerly known as NECC), ISTE represents more than 100,000 professionals worldwide. We support our members with information, networking opportunities, and guidance as they face the challenge of transforming education. To find out more about these and other ISTE initiatives, visit our website at www.iste.org.

As part of our mission, ISTE Book Publishing works with experienced educators to develop and produce practical resources for classroom teachers, teacher educators, and technology leaders. Every manuscript we select for publication is carefully peer-reviewed and professionally edited. We value your feedback on this book and other ISTE products. E-mail us at books@iste.org.

Contact Us

Washington, DC, Office:
   1710 Rhode Island Ave. NW, Suite 900, Washington, DC 20036-3132
Eugene, Oregon, Office:
   180 West 8th Ave., Suite 300, Eugene, OR 97401-2916
Order Desk: 1.800.336.5191
Order Fax: 1.541.302.3778
Customer Service: orders@iste.org
Book Publishing: books@iste.org
Book Sales and Marketing: booksmarketing@iste.org
Web: www.iste.org

Think outside the box!

Camille Cole (signature)

About the Author

Camille Cole is a thirty-year educator who has worked both in the classroom and as the coordinator of distance learning for the State of Oregon. She now works full-time as an educational program development consultant and grant writer.

During Camille's tenure as the distance learning program manager for K–12 Oregon, 1998–2006, she oversaw the deployment and implementation of Oregon's statewide videoconference network, *Oregon Access Network*. She has been a national leader in the K–12 educational technology field for over 20 years. Camille is the president and principal researcher for Schoolhouse Communications, an e-learning and technology implementation consulting and communications group. She is an alumna of the University of Oregon's School of Education.

Camille is the coauthor of *Videoconferencing for K–12 Classrooms*, (ISTE, 2009), which is used worldwide in university classrooms, teacher training workshops, and seminars. She also writes historical non-fiction and fiction. Her work has been published in literary and professional journals. She is currently working on the educational history book *The Brass Bell*.

You can find out more about Camille's work at www.camillecole.com

Thanks and Recognition

I'd like to thank the people who took the time from their busy schedules to be interviewed for this book: Dr. Patricia Galloway, Mowgli Holmes, Dr. Laurence Peters, Kathy Schrock, and Dr. Lynn Schrum. Also, thanks to my family for their support and encouragement. Finally, special thanks to Jay Matheson for his inspiration and support when I needed it most.

Dedication

For my parents, Peter Wilcox Cole and Ethel McPherson Cole

Contents

Chapter 6

Funding Ideas

Chapter 7

Tools, Tactics, Take Off! Web 2.0 Resources

Conclusion

Appendix

National Educational Technology Standards

References

Index

Introduction

This is the digital generation—a generation of kids raised in a media-rich, networked world of infinite possibilities. ... They are learning, communicating and socializing in new and exciting ways. ... For them, technology is more than just a tool, it's an essential component of everyday life that frames their world view.

But there's more to their world than just playing with gadgets. It's about engagement, self-directed learning, creativity, and empowerment. They are hyperconnected to their friends and family, mastering new tools and techniques with ease. Behind every successful kid are adults and peers who guide, motivate, and support them.

—EDUTOPIA, THE DIGITAL GENERATION PROJECT

STEM = Science, Technology, Engineering, and Math

When the Soviets launched Sputnik in 1957, school kids waited in their backyards at night to get a glimpse of the first satellite as it blinked across a star-filled sky. The advent of the space age brought about a short-term boost in the awareness and popularity of STEM curriculum and careers. American newspaper headlines warned about the "science gap" between the U.S. and the U.S.S.R. STEM professionals such as Wernher von Braun, Chuck Yeager, John Glenn, and even NASA staffers became pop culture icons. STEM's place in education and culture seemed to be assured.

Unfortunately, as with most things, the media attention eventually died down. Ironically, in today's world, although there are more possibilities for STEM careers, more need for them, and more choices in them than ever before, the percentage of students pursuing STEM-related degrees has declined.

Increasing student interest in STEM is a high priority for schools. It has been identified as a focus by most prominent educational systems worldwide. Although making STEM a priority is a strong first step, without strategies for making these curriculum areas interesting and attractive to students, STEM initiatives are doomed to fail.

In this book I offer educational leaders a vision for educational reform—with ideas that won't break your budget. By using the latest technologies, including Web 2.0 tools, to expose students to, and build their interest in, STEM curriculum areas and careers, educators can increase the popularity of STEM studies even among the youngest students.

We cannot afford to wait around for the next big breakthrough or the next perceived crisis to bring attention back to this area. Students need to be exposed to more than vague media stereotypes that STEM curriculum areas are only for nerds. Students need authentic engagement with professionals working in these fields. Many students have no real connection to an adult in a STEM career. It can be almost impossible for such a student to imagine herself as a scientist, engineer, technician, or mathematician when she has never met anyone who works in those fields.

Used effectively, career awareness can lead to highly successful strategies for engaging students in the STEM areas. This book offers a glimpse into some of today's successful classrooms, describing innovative projects in which students are connected to real-world professionals. These examples and the related lists of resources and tools can be powerful aids in helping kids discover and pursue their STEM talents, passions, and careers.

Unfortunately, we all know that there is often little money for visits to museums, to meet role models, to spend time with peers in other cultures, or to take field trips to regional science centers. Even when grants or other funding is available, access to public and private labs and the professionals who work in them is often limited or impractical.

Web 2.0 technologies offer solutions to both budget-challenged and physically isolated schools. With the advent of these new digital communication and collaboration technologies and the proliferation of broadband networks in schools, students now can have access to meaningful hands-on experiences around the globe with professionals of every stripe. They can build relationships, discover new career opportunities, and have experiences that inform them about a world far beyond their borders. We no longer have to exist in isolated communities or allow a lack of funding to hold our students back. Many educators are discovering all kinds of ways to connect to the outside world without leaving the classroom. In this book, we look at the possibilities, the successes, and the challenges.

Young people are passionate. They want to participate, and they want to make the world a better place—but it can be difficult for them to envision possibilities without role models and real-life examples. We have a landmark opportunity to help make connections between students and the STEM community. When students can meet and develop relationships with role models and career coaches in fields they have never envisioned, their potential and motivation expands exponentially.

The Importance of STEM

Wait a minute. Why, you ask, are science, technology, engineering, and math so important? To answer this, all you need to do is think about how radically our world and lives have changed in the past 10 years compared to the last 200 years, and the previous millennium.

Consider this: at the beginning of the 20th century, 38% of the labor force was needed for farm work. Today, in part because of the industrialization of farming, the farm labor force constitutes less than 3% of the population. On the 2000 U.S. Census report's trade listing, farming (or farm labor) was not even listed as a sector of the labor force for the country. This is just one example of how the workforce has dramatically changed.

The Bureau of Labor Statistics has reported that science and engineering occupations are projected to grow by 21.4% from 2004 to 2014, compared to a growth of 13% in all occupations during the same time period. Approximately 65% of the growth in these occupations will be in computer-related occupations (Matthews, 2007).

According to the Institute for a Competitive Workforce (2008), the very nature of America's economy has changed dramatically over the past decade and will continue to do so. In a knowledge-based, innovation-driven era, different knowledge, skills, and abilities will be required for workers and employers to be successful. The new workplace demands higher-order technical knowledge, as well as universally necessary skills such as the ability to learn on one's own; to gather and synthesize information; to work effectively in teams; to solve problems; to communicate through multiple means; and to manage time, money, and responsibilities.

STEM careers now encompass millions of jobs in a wide range of career tracks and occupations—jobs that call for innovative, highly trained scientists, mathematicians, and engineers. STEM workers address critical world problems and produce much-needed and innovative advances in renewable energy, climate science, public health, communications, transportation, and national security—to name a just few. More and more, jobs of the future—and not just jobs in the STEM fields—will require a foundation in math, science, engineering, and technology.

In the 2010 Lemelson-MIT Invention Index (Survey, 2010), which gauges Americans' perceptions about invention and innovation, as many as 77% of high school students demonstrated an interest in pursuing a STEM career. However, in a recent survey inspired by President Obama's "Educate to Innovate" campaign and conducted by the market research firm Harris Interactive, 63% of high school students said their teachers are not doing a good job of talking to them about engineering careers, and 42% said teachers also do not do a good job of demonstrating how science can be used in a career.

To be fair, how in the world are teachers, with all they have to accomplish, to know about the ever-changing world of work, and about the numerous jobs in the hundreds of career tracks in the STEM fields? This is why it's so important to make the connection between the classroom and professionals in the workplace. Technology makes it possible.

The Global Economy and STEM Careers

Are schools keeping up? Are they following a track that will introduce students to fields of study and ultimately qualifications and careers that allow them to solve the kinds of social and environmental problems we are dealing with more and more: massive oil spills, global warming, widespread communicable and degenerative diseases, obesity, transportation and infrastructure issues, and the ever-looming energy crisis? Today's young people will inherit issues that will demand a team effort and a global response, involving large numbers of people all over the world who have been trained at many different levels in science, technology, engineering, and mathematics. These issues will also require people who are creative and artistic and are able to think critically and work collaboratively within a global framework.

To gain entrance into the world that awaits them, to be prepared, students need access to tools that will help them acquire a global perspective now. The rising globalization of the economy calls for the globalization of education. It calls for students who understand cultures other than their own and understand the context in which they learn. To do this, students need access to collaborative and productive digital tools that put them in touch with professionals at home and abroad.

As students reach out to professionals and peers internationally, they build an awareness of other cultures, learn about global issues, and create partnerships with peers and role models. They can use digital media tools such as videoconferencing, webcasting, blogging, and social networking to explore a larger world.

The New Classroom

The Horizon Report (Johnson, Levine, Smith, & Smythe, 2009), covering a study launched in 2002, *The Horizon Project*, summarizing dialogues with hundreds of technology professionals, school technologists, educators, and representatives of leading corporations from more than two-dozen countries, concludes that:

> Schools are still using materials developed to teach the students of decades ago, but today's students are actually very different in the way they think and work. Schools need to adapt to current student needs and identify new learning models that are engaging to younger generations. Many education professionals feel that a shift to a more learner-centered model focused on the development of individual potential instead of the imposition of a body of knowledge would lead to deeper and more sustainable learning across the curriculum. To support such a change, both teaching practice and the tools used in the classroom must adapt.... Students are seeking some connection between their own lives and their experience in school. Use of technology tools that are already familiar to students, project-based learning practices that incorporate real-life experiences, and

mentoring from community members are a few practices that support increased engagement. ... However, making such a profound shift in a well-established system is a difficult challenge. Professional development, intellectual interactions with peers, adequate training, and preparation time—all scarce resources for teachers—are necessary in abundance for such a shift to take place. (p. 7)

Educators must transform their schools and the ways they teach. Students need to be encouraged and allowed to interact regularly and significantly with professionals, experts, mentors, and role models, particularly in the STEM fields. When students engage with passionate practitioners, they can begin to see their own potential careers and motivation is significantly increased.

> **A LEARNER-CENTERED** classroom with an emphasis on project-based lessons is a fundamental assumption throughout this book.

A learner-centered classroom with an emphasis on project-based lessons is a fundamental assumption throughout this book. We look at this concept in depth in Chapter 1. The responsibility of creating and nurturing a classroom environment where students can explore and connect with multiple topics and mentors lies with the entire educational system, including teachers, administrators, policy makers, parents, and the community.

The
New Classroom

The most important thing is to engage your mind in something that's important.

—Mark Prensky

As I mentioned in the Introduction, a learner-centered classroom with an emphasis on project-based lessons is a fundamental assumption throughout this book. I call this way of teaching the "new classroom." In some ways, students already have access to the environment of my proposed new classroom. Young people are already connecting and learning in new ways that are both collective and egalitarian. Often they are doing this outside the classroom on their own time. They are plugged into social networks that define, in some ways, who they are. On Facebook, MySpace, and YouTube, they build communities of friends with shared passions. They are mostly doing this without the guidance of their schools, teachers, or parents.

Educators must explore ways to engage students in their learning with the same Web 2.0 applications their students already eagerly use outside the classroom. To fully capitalize on the potential, we need to rethink what a "typical" educational environment should look like. I'd like to offer you my vision of what the ideal "STEM-empowered" classroom could look like. Of course, the technologies that bring STEM into the classroom could be applied to almost any subject—and should be!

A Classroom of the Future

Jump into my time machine as we journey into the future and observe a typical classroom. What class or subject? you ask. This classroom is designed specifically for particular types of project work, so students are here today because of the projects they are working on and the teams to which they belong, rather than for specific content-based learning.

Notice that there are clusters of learners in several different areas, called learning stations. Right away, we can see several projectors fixed to the ceiling, and various sizes of screens throughout the room. Interactive white boards line the walls between the projection screens.

One group of students is huddled over one of several worktables available throughout the room. If you look closer, you'll notice that the tables have wheels—the room can easily be reconfigured at will. Students, heads together, hover over their tablets and laptops. They are engaged in an animated conversation, and they scribble and type furiously.

Another student group near the side wall examines images on a small, wall-mounted LCD screen. They have pushed their worktable and chairs close to the screen.

At the other end of the classroom, a teacher monitors a dashboard on a podium-like station. She has been gathering snapshots of information and feedback from each of the learning stations. Now she walks toward three students who are lying back on what look like dental chairs. They each wear virtual-reality goggles and are viewing 3-D images of giant orca whales and pods of dolphin at the Mote Marine Laboratory in Florida (www.mote.org/seatrek). These students are investigating careers in marine biology. One is actually on a virtual voyage with a marine biologist. They are exploring the ocean floor. This student is passionate about the health of the planet's oceans and very excited to experience what a marine biologist does.

Everywhere you look in this sizable classroom, students are involved in groups. Some group members are present via videoconference from distant locations. There are remote professionals available from whom students receive coaching and guidance. In this ideal future, it has become standard for professionals in STEM fields, and other fields, to collaborate with students in primary and secondary schools—a sort of career internship. Classroom teachers arrange and facilitate the partnerships. You can see that the remote instructors are in laboratories, space stations, and even an operating room in a hospital in China. Classroom teachers wander throughout the classroom, checking on team progress, answering technology questions, and keeping students on task.

When we look more closely at the physical space, we see document cameras, wireless tablets, and various multimedia materials. Every 15 feet or so there is a computer monitor with a webcam. Teachers authorize access to websites throughout the day.

> **WE HAVE AMPLE PROOF** that an incremental approach in which the future is seen as an extrapolation of the past is doomed for failure. So the question for us is now to set the stage for the future by growing the opportunities for shared group experiences. We have the capacity today (holodeck or not) to let teachers and students co-create and explore shared spaces where we can all learn together. … Our current classroom technology can be harnessed to facilitate virtual field trips. While not quite as cool as the full holodeck, these experiences support different kinds of learning, and should be explored.
>
> —David Thornburg (1994, p. 2)

Students are free to leave the classroom and research in the field. They are always connected to a teacher through a handheld device. They are able to produce and share both audio and video from their handhelds. The handhelds are assigned to students as part of their school membership.

Project teams chronicle their work in e-portfolios, with each student contributing assigned portions of the portfolio. The results are presented locally and virtually at the project's completion.

Welcome back to the present! It may take many years to get to the scenario that we just explored, and it's a given that the future will be somewhat different from what we imagine—but without a vision of what we're striving for, it is all but impossible to begin. Yes, today's average classroom does not look much like the classroom of the future, but the good news is, technology can help us take a giant step in that direction. Our combined knowledge, creativity, and courage will help shape the classrooms of the future. The outcome is still in our hands.

Emerging Innovative Classrooms

The New Media Consortium's 2009 Horizon Report states, "Traditionally, a learning environment has been a physical space, but the idea of what constitutes a learning environment is changing. The 'spaces' where students learn are becoming more community-driven, interdisciplinary, and supported by technologies that engage virtual communication and collaboration" (Johnson et al, 2009, p. 6). You saw several examples of this during our visit to the future classroom. Although these innovations are not necessarily STEM-specific, the potential to connect students to environments and communities where they can be exposed to STEM professionals and careers is obvious.

Can we find leadership in the innovative classroom movement? Yes! Next we'll look at a few innovative programs that are moving toward the type of classrooms where my vision for STEM education might flourish.

Pennsylvania Classrooms of the Future

With the largest statewide educational technology initiative in the country, Pennsylvania has spent more than $200 million between 2006 and 2011 to fully equip classrooms with Internet-connected laptops, electronic whiteboards, and other peripheral equipment in 90% of the high schools in the state. A substantial focus of the program was on providing part-time teacher coaches and embedded professional development. As of this writing, the project has touched about 550 high schools, 12,000 teachers, and 500,000 students.

Edward G. Rendell, who was governor of the state until January 2011, implemented the Classrooms of the Future grant program initiative and spoke frankly about students falling behind, ill-prepared for the global marketplace. He made it his mission to make sure the students of his state would be successful in an ever-expanding, high-tech global marketplace. As a result, teachers have been given a chance, says one Pennsylvania principal, to rethink how they design learning environments and strategies—to change the way they develop instruction.

With a focus on the core subjects (math, science, English and social studies), the Classrooms for the Future program equips math and science classrooms with the technology and support for teachers to incorporate STEM into their teaching. It is with these seemingly small steps that schools will go forward and implement instruction in a way that provides for curriculum partnerships with professionals in the STEM fields. With the embedded teacher training, teachers will eventually use technology to connect students to role models and mentors in science, technology, engineering, and mathematics. Programs such as Classrooms for the Future are based on a growth and development model with an eye on results 10 years from now and beyond. While teachers gain confidence today, students gain ongoing support and guidance in the use of digital media, preparing them for what lies ahead in a world that changes every day with each new technological development.

> **WE CANNOT PREPARE** the "Technology Generation" to be the innovators, leaders and entrepreneurs of the 21st century using chalk and blackboards. Classrooms for the Future will not only help boost achievement while students are still in high school, but also help prepare them for success in college and beyond, especially in fields that require advanced skills with computers and technology.
>
> —*Classrooms for the Future Grant Program Arrives in Harrisburg, PA. (Government Technology, 2008)*

The Digital Youth Network

Based on the research of Brigid Barron, associate professor of education at Stanford University, and Kimberley Gomez, associate professor of education at the University of Pittsburgh, the Digital Youth Network is a Chicago-based digital literacy program connecting inner-city students with mentors online. The online portion of the project is modeled after social media sites such as Facebook and MySpace and is called Remix World.

The Digital Youth Network provides a blended, or hybrid, program for students in which they can engage in learning environments in and out of school, learning new media literacies and applying them to communicate and collaborate in meaningful ways. The idea of the program is to reach students on both sides of the classroom walls, at any time of the day.

Middle school students, Grades 6–8, partner with high school and career-based digital mentors to learn to use social media and other popular digital tools responsibly and effectively.

According to the program's website (http://digitalyouthnetwork.org), "The combination of in-school and out-of-school programming simultaneously provides a base of knowledge to allow in-school teachers to embed digital literacy into instruction without fear of having to teach kids how to use the new media tools."

NING IS A SOCIAL NETWORKING SITE. Nings have borrowed the tools and the format of Facebook, MySpace, and other lesser-known social networking sites. A Ning lets you create and join social networks dedicated and formed around a particular area of interest, such as implementing digital media in the classroom. Ning features include blogs, forums, status feeds, and event feeds. They also include the playful elements of any social networking site, such as personal profiles, pictures, and avatars. A Ning is more interactive than simply reading materials online. There is a strong human element, and relationships can be formed with cohorts around the world.

Ning has recently begun charging fees for many features. Though the fee is nominal, many classrooms cannot afford the cost of online subscriptions of any kind. As might be expected, a plethora of free Ning replacement applications have emerged and will continue to emerge. I suggest you will find the most current information by conducting a web-search for free Ning replacements.

The program was funded by the John D. and Catherine T. MacArthur Foundation. Students attend school during the day and meet once a week for two hours in groups called "pods." They use an online forum as a place to share work and get feedback from mentors, learning through trial and error and the connections and conversations that occur after hours and after publication.

Program Director Akili Lee reported on the Edutopia website that educators can draw valuable lessons about how to exploit social networking for more formal learning:

> Social networking is the platform they're used to. It is a very sophisticated communication platform and, in many ways, it's a collaborative platform. If they're communicating and collaborating in a certain way, why can't we leverage that?

Program leaders encourage other teachers to use Ning, the social network creation site (see Ning is a Social Networking Site on previous page), to develop their own student collaboration networks. One of the Digital Youth Network students agrees. "It's better to create your own," he told Edutopia writer Laila Weir. "You can build social networks around the curriculum, so you can use them as a teaching resource or another tool" (Edutopia, 2010). The advantage of this tool, almost everyone would agree, is that nearly every student on the planet is already using social media in one way or another to communicate and collaborate. If you can harness that enthusiasm and that resource—adopt the tool and adapt to the tool—imagine what you might be able to accomplish as an educator.

The Digital Youth Network is an example of how providing digital communication tools can establish a platform for developing partnerships with mentors in scientific fields—from health care to university research projects. Students and STEM mentors are able to develop an online community where they can collaborate in real time and share resources. Mentors can introduce students to their professional environments, talk to them about what they do in the course of a day. Students who are interested can learn how these mentors were able to succeed in school to become STEM professionals.

This is an efficient means of bringing role models to the classroom. No one has to travel, take time off from school or work, and the relationship can be ongoing. This is also a perfect example of how adults in the workplace can participate in school improvement, can donate their time and expertise without much interruption of their workday.

INTERVIEW

Kathy Schrock

Kathy Schrock is the director of technology for the Nauset Public Schools on Cape Cod, Massachusetts. A large part of her job deals with embedding technology throughout the curriculum in all areas and at all grade levels. Previously a library media specialist, she is very interested in search strategies, evaluation of Internet information, copyright issues, emerging technologies and gadgets, and the use of technology as a tool to support instruction. Kathy is also an Adobe Education Leader, a Google Certified Teacher, and a Discovery STAR Educator.

Camille: I understand that you just received a Thinkfinity grant for a STEM project for Grades 7 and 8. So many educators are now focusing on the importance of STEM education and career awareness in the STEM fields. What is your take on this trend?

Kathy: I feel the STEM initiative, by bundling science, technology, engineering, and mathematics together, provides a more meaningful way for teachers to develop units and lessons, as well as a coordinated approach for students to conduct project-based learning activities. What engineering lesson does not involve math or scientific principles?

Camille: Can you tell me about your project and why you selected Grades 7 and 8 as a target group?

Kathy: The grant I recently received focuses solely on the manufacturing process for Grades 7 and 8. The students are introduced to more than 100 manufacturing processes that, hopefully, will provide them with some background information for their future career choice path. In seventh grade, the students will conduct research on various manufacturing processes (information literacy), work in collaborative Google Docs groups to plan a presentation (technology literacy), create a presentation (presentation skills), and present to the group (communication skills). The eighth graders will continue by creating their own product, researching the competitive products, and creating a one-minute commercial for their product. All aspects of these two units seamlessly embed technology, Web 2.0 apps, and information literacy skills in the project-based learning. They also include, of course, the importance of manufacturing and global initiatives as the world economy shifts its focus.

Camille: With teachers working so hard to keep up with mandates, growing class size, and so on, what are the best strategies for teachers in schools where there is not strong leadership to keep up with the STEM initiatives?

Kathy: It has always been my feeling that interdisciplinary units are the most meaningful for students and provide the teacher with the ability to cover multiple content standards and benchmarks in a single unit. STEM-based units lend themselves to this type of planning and teaching. There are also many online repositories of information and lesson plans available on the web in the area of STEM education. In addition, teachers in these schools should cultivate a personal learning network of educators who are active and knowledgeable in this area. They might find them on Twitter (by searching on Twitter for "#STEM"), by searching Ning (by simply searching STEM), or by attending educational STEM organizations' conferences (such as AAAS, AERA, AECT, ISTE, NARST, NCTM, NSTA, etc.)

In this chapter we visited a STEM-empowered classroom of the future and touched on innovative programs that are moving in that direction today. Now let's dive deeper into ways to increase STEM career awareness in our students.

Chapter 2

What Is
Career Awareness?

No wind favors him who has no destined port.
—Montaigne

WHAT DO STUDENTS KNOW about the possibilities in the professional world that lies ahead? In their daily lives, students typically encounter adults in a somewhat limited variety of professions—perhaps their parents, their teachers, doctors, store clerks, bus drivers, and so on. They see characters in multiple professions on television and in movies, but how realistic are the portrayals? In day-to-day life, few students interact in meaningful ways with professionals in STEM careers.

As a child, did you ever have the chance to chat with a mechanical engineer? An astronaut? A neurologist? Students probably know in an intellectual way that these are career choices, but without role models or direct interactions, the path to these careers probably seems unclear and daunting.

For the context of this book, career awareness for primary and secondary students is an understanding of the existence of and the requirements for a wide array of professions in science, technology, engineering, and mathematics. Students may be passionate about social and environmental issues, but without career awareness, most likely they will remain unaware of how these interests might translate into a STEM career or job. Building relationships with professionals fosters career awareness, which in turn motivates students to work. Schoolwork is more interesting, authentic, and rewarding because they know why they are doing it.

STUDENTS' UNDERSTANDING of the world of work can be enriched as they identify career pathways, specific occupations within those pathways, and meet and develop relationships with real-life professionals. Students might discover new passions and interests as they get an up-close look at a working scientist or engineer. In some cases, students who have given up on school begin to envision a future.

—*Center of Science and Industry (COSI, www.cosi.org)*

What could be more personally meaningful than building relationships with astronauts who have spent months on the space station, with a research scientist trying to find a cure for AIDS, with a deep sea explorer, or with a paleontologist who has discovered bones of a new species of dinosaur? When students make these connections, the first thing they are interested in is the person. They begin a relationship with an adult unlike any they have met before. They want to know more about their lives. Often they want to be like them. This is the beginning of career awareness.

Once students develop an interest in a certain career path, the next step is to make a connection with their own lives. High school students need access to current, comprehensive, and in-depth information about careers. They need to be aware of details such as typical duties and tasks, what a day in the life of a person in that career is like, and what kinds of employment projections for hiring and wages currently exist for that position or that career.

Students are often interested in and inspired by issues. Students might be interested in global warming or health-related issues but not know how to translate those interests into a meaningful career. How should they prepare while in secondary school, what should they study in college, and in the end, what jobs would be open to them? Without exposure to an array of professionals, science centers, museums, and laboratories, how would they know?

Students who were once isolated within the four walls of the classroom can now easily use interactive digital media and distance learning tools to interview professionals and to learn from role models through firsthand experiences. As students develop relationships with a mentor or guest speaker with whom they interact through communications technologies, they are likely to develop an interest in, or at least a curiosity about, the field that adult represents. Such relationships make learning and goal setting more authentic for students. They begin to understand the education and training needed to fulfill their dreams.

> **THERE'S A NATURAL** curiosity that young people have—because in their minds they're going to be doing some of those things. You never know when you're going to come across an interest in a child. Let's try and give kids as many options as we can about when that interest might get challenged—and relationships start to develop.
>
> —*Jay Matheson, director of the Extending Career Options for Rural Students project*

An extensive listing of STEM-designated degree programs is available at www.ice.gov/sevis/stemlist.htm. When students research these careers tracks, they can find out what jobs fall under each heading. For a career-awareness activity, perhaps they could locate and interview someone whose job fits into one of these categories. The relationship between a student and a professional in a STEM field can be as simple as an email interview or a one-time videoconference or web conference, or as extensive as a yearlong mentorship relationship.

INTERVIEW

Mowgli Holmes

Mowgli Holmes is the son of a friend of mine. He is working on his PhD at Columbia University. His research project involves HIV inoculation. His undergraduate work was at Vassar, and like most young college students he focused on liberal arts and philosophy. For a time after graduation he seemed to flounder, playing drums in a band. Then he surprised everyone by taking up graduate courses in engineering at a state university. I decided I'd talk to him, hoping to get some insight into what interested him and motivated him to pursue this work, a path that no one, including him, thought he might explore. He was quick to respond to my request for an interview, and here is a snippet of our conversation.

Camille: When did you first become interested in science or engineering as a career path?

Mowgli: I didn't become interested in science as a career path until I had been out of school for five years. I had no background whatsoever in the sciences, but had been reading pop science books and became a little obsessed with some of the new theoretical biology work that people were doing. Plus, I needed a job.

Camille: Was there a pivotal experience or relationship that motivated you to pursue the research, the study, you are currently pursuing?

Mowgli: Yes. I suddenly realized that my undergrad degree in philosophy was never going to let me support myself. But also, I have some friends with HIV and it made sense to me to work on a problem that was not abstract. Now I work in an HIV lab.

Camille: Did you ever feel unprepared for the requirements of graduate education?

Mowgli: I was totally unprepared—I had never taken a math or science course in my whole undergraduate education. But I was well prepared to read, write, and learn stuff quickly, so I took background courses at the local state school before applying to a graduate program, and that was enough.

Camille: Tell me about the goals of your research and how did you come upon them?

Mowgli: The goals of my PhD research are to find a way to test HIV vaccines in mice, but mice are immune to HIV. I got to this because I was very goal-oriented when I began grad school— I just wanted to solve this problem we had: 40 million people with HIV. We probably won't have a vaccine any time soon unless we can engineer a way to test it in mice.

Camille: Will you pursue a career path related to your research?

Mowgli: Probably. Though scientists are extraordinarily rigid, much of the time, and if I can switch to some kind of art/science interface I will probably do it. An artist friend and I have started a bio-art collective, and we're still using science—but our goals and approaches are much more fluid. I like that.

There actually is a tremendous need for info on the web about the nuts and bolts of different careers. As of right now, that info is not very good, and not very accessible. Doing basic searches about different careers, such as mechanical engineer or microbiologist, usually yields mainly inscrutable job listings. You also get university websites with handy paragraphs for their undergrads, trying to give a brief description of what they can expect with this or that major. The Bureau of Labor Statistics has interesting info on every single career, but it's a bit dry to say the least. What you don't find, at least not yet, is much of the kind of interactive experience that you're talking about here—windows into what it's actually like to do different jobs, or to work in a lab, and so on. There's a bewildering array of microspecialties out there these days, and before you dive into them, they're all basically black boxes. So I hope the kind of thing you're writing about really comes to life.

Mowgli's example of an early academic experience unfocused on career opportunity is very common. Although he was fortunate enough to find his passion and interests shortly after he earned his undergraduate degree, that isn't common.

Most agree that one of the best ways to learn is through hands-on experiences and investigation. Participatory, digital media tools provide opportunities for direct interaction with role models who can provide inspiration by the example of their own lives and experiences. A question-and-answer session with an engineer who's a woman, an astronaut who's black, or a researcher who's physically challenged says to students: Don't let anyone ever tell you that you are not qualified or not capable of following your aspirations in any career field, no matter what.

CAREER AWARENESS focuses on using a variety of resources to introduce students to a broad range of career options.... Career awareness at the elementary and middle school levels helps expand student understanding of the world of work by identifying career pathways and specific occupations within them, developing respect for workers in all fields, locating and researching information about specific occupations, and developing an understanding of educational and training requirements. Continuing this awareness process, high school students need to be provided current, comprehensive, and in-depth information about careers, including detailed descriptions of typical duties, responsibilities, and tasks; projections on employment openings; and understanding of working conditions, current income and benefit ranges, educational requirements and opportunities, and opportunities for advancement.... Career awareness activities also provide students with a better understanding of the changing nature of careers due to technological advances, the impact of a global economy, and the anticipation of the need for individuals to change careers several times during the course of a lifetime.

—*Office of Career and Technical Education, Michigan Department of Education (www.michigan.gov)*

For a child in the fifth grade, for example, who has discovered a passion for nature and the environment, career awareness activities could include meeting professionals who work in related fields. A report from *Science* (Pain & Carpenter, 2009) says that "Opportunities are expanding for natural and social scientists who wish to take on the scientific and practical challenges posed by climate change.... If early-career scientists 'embark on careers in this field today, they will only find greater and greater excitement as they progress.' "

Imagine the impact on this fifth grader if he or she were able to interact with a research scientist in the climate change field and learn about the different pathways available to one day study and work in this field. Better yet, what if the student could build a relationship with this scientist and he or she became someone the student looked up to and wanted to emulate? This student might well develop a focus in his or her studies quite early on.

> **STUDENTS HAVE** a natural curiosity about adults.
>
> —*Jay Matheson*

Career Awareness at All Grade Levels

I've mentioned over and over that the latest digital technologies, and especially Web 2.0 tools, make connecting students to STEM career resources quite easy. I'll get into these technologies in depth in Chapter 7, here I briefly touch on how the tools might be used at various grade levels.

Elementary students might use interactive videoconferencing as a virtual textbook—observing professionals at work in museums, science centers, or universities. Virtual field-trip content providers often give participating students opportunities to ask questions about the featured jobs and about the fields of study required.

Middle school students might use digital technologies as a virtual guide or mentor, exploring career options in STEM fields. Partnerships and mentoring relationships can be formed and nurtured throughout a school year using inter-active videoconferencing, Web 2.0 communication tools, classroom Nings, and blogs. Again, the idea is to introduce students early on to career and occupational information through examples of real people working in real jobs.

High school students might use digital communication and collaboration tools, such as web dialogues, as a virtual career counselor, extending state-mandated career experiences with virtual job shadowing and mock interviews. Web dialogues can be arranged with graduate students and seasoned professionals. Partnerships and role models are powerful motivators.

Research shows that early career exploration, proactive career planning, the involvement of at least one caring adult, and a wealth of information about educational requirements and job opportunities in the labor market all dramatically increase a young person's chances of obtaining and retaining a successful career pathway that leads to adult self-sufficiency.

Although STEM professionals work in a wide variety of fields and locations, some good areas to find and connect with people that are likely to have a high degree of interest in working with students are:

- Museums

- Science and technology centers

- Zoos

- Botanical gardens

- Teaching hospitals and research centers

Career Awareness Resources

I hope that you are now energized about the possibilities inherent in increasing your students' career awareness. You may be feeling a little overwhelmed and wondering where to begin. I've compiled here a list of resources to inspire you and help you dive in immediately.

American Institute of Biological Sciences
www.aibs.org/careers

> The institute is a professional organization for the advancement of biological research and education. The career site is set up with an information dialogue explaining how interesting and rewarding a career in this field can be. Questions include "What does a biologist do?" and "How can I prepare for a career in biology?" The home page includes links to lists of careers in biology, job openings, and professional meetings; discusses ways in which students in Grades K–12 can get involved, including student membership; and links to a Students in Biology Facebook page.

American Mathematical Society
www.ams.org/employment/highschool.html

> This site contains everything you ever needed or wanted to know if you are interested in mathematics: mathematics help and resources; math clubs and events; online magazines, posters, competitions and contests; and of course, a careers page.

American Society of Mechanical Engineers—Early Career Engineers Center
www.asme.org/Communities/EarlyCareer/

This career center offers videos, e-mentoring, graduate student resources, leadership training, conferences, grant opportunities, and white papers. This site would be ideal for high school juniors and seniors entering an engineering program or interested in exploring the field (at any grade level).

Association of Medical Illustrators
www.ami.org

As you might imagine, this site is graphically exciting, and the rotating illustrations of arteries and vessels and cells are breathtaking. At the toolbar across the top of the page, hover over Medical Illustration and then click on Careers. I tell you this so students don't miss the front page. The Careers page provides detailed information about what a medical illustrator is, what skills and education the career requires, what its earning potential is, and so on.

Bureau of Labor Statistics
http://stats.bls.gov/k12

This website for kids provides introductory career information for students in Grades 4–8 and has been adapted from the bureau's *Occupational Outlook Handbook* for high school students and adults. The website provides graphic portals to career fields organized according to interest, including science and nature. The language is simplified, and a teacher guide is included.

Career Key
www.careerkey.org

The Career Key site provides a wealth of information about career pathways, exploration activities, and required job skills. The author of the site is a career counselor; the site is geared to the high school level.

Connect a Million Minds
www.connectamillionminds.com

In April 2009, Time Warner Cable, along with the National Science Foundation and the White House, announced a business–education partnership to bring STEM career and education resources to U.S. schoolchildren. The media company committed $100 million cash and in-kind domations to inspire students to pursue STEM careers. The initiative is anchored by a participatory website for students, teachers, partners, and parents, and seeks to gain the participation of communities, schools, and businesses around the country.

In an ongoing effort to inform and engage the public, President Obama, in November 2009, called for business and nonprofit leaders to participate in the program. "Lifting American students from the middle to the top of the pack in STEM achievement over the next decade will not be attained by government alone" (Time Warner Cable, 2009).

In January 2010, President Obama announced an expansion of the program, called Educate to Innovate, expanding the partnerships of the original program to include Intel's Science and Math Teachers Initiative, an expansion of the National Math and Science Initiative's UTeach Program; 75 major public universities; PBS Innovative Educators Challenge; and the Woodrow Wilson Teaching Fellowships in Math and Science.

The president said, "I am calling on all 200,000 scientists who work for the federal government to do their part in their communities: to speak to schools, to create hands-on learning opportunities ... and to help stoke that same curiosity in students which perhaps led them to pursue a career in science in the first place" (Prabhu, 2010)

In an ongoing effort to keep the program in the forefront and to meet the goals of a five-year $100 million effort, Time Warner Cable hosted a second annual Connect a Million Minds (CAMM) Week in April 2011.

During year one of the program, more than 3,000 students and Time Warner Cable employee volunteers participated in an inaugural launch week, which included the support of 24 partners in 8 states.

Engineer Girl
www.engineergirl.org

This is a fun site, featuring role models and students, contests, fun facts, links, great achievements, and serious information about various fields of engineering and their requirements. My favorite was the page with profiles of women engineers.

Engineer Your Life
www.engineeryourlife.org

This website is a guide to engineering careers for high school girls, providing resources such as role model videos and information for counselors and other advisors. The site is produced in cooperation with the National Academy of Engineering.

NASA

www.nasa.gov/audience/forstudents/careers-index.html

NASA has an extensive site for educators. Their career page provides a variety of ways kids can learn about jobs at NASA and meet scientists, engineers, mathematicians, physicists, astronauts, and astronomers. NASA offers internships, visiting faculty, profiles of NASA employees, job descriptions at NASA, and career information posters for the classroom. Career content is sorted by grade level.

National Institutes of Health (NIH) Office of Science Education

http://science.education.nih.gov/home2.nsf/Careers/Career+Exploration

This career site provides lists of health-career pathways and job descriptions within those pathways. The site offers supporting educational resources by grade level. A Women in Science section showcases successful female scientists. Students can find out about educational requirements and available options in these specialties, as well as discover how women have influenced the field of medicine.

National Institutes of Health (NIH)
Office of Science Education, LifeWorks Project

www.science.education.nih.gov/lifeworks

Explore health and medical science careers. The database is organized alphabetically or by areas of interest, salary categories, and education requirements. On the lighter side, students meet dentists, doctors, and other health and medical science professionals through interview materials posted and rotated to keep students who are interested coming back for more.

Open Source Teaching Project

www.opensourceteaching.org

This free program offers a forum where students can interview successful professionals, helping to inspire and inform students at all levels as they make their education and career decisions. The digital platform is available for K–20 students. The project actively recruits people to share life and career experiences using social media tools.

Science Careers

http://sciencecareers.sciencemag.org

At this website, sponsored by the journal *Science*, there is a wealth of resources, from articles to job search databases, magazines, and job and career tips. This site alone will open young eyes to all kinds of opportunities in many different worlds.

Sloan Career Cornerstone Center

www.careercornerstone.org

This career exploration site focuses specifically on science, technology, engineering, mathematics, computing, and health care. Podcast interviews with professionals are available for students to watch any time.

STEMtube

www.STEMtube.com

An online warehouse for student projects.

United States Department of Agriculture

www.nal.usda.gov

For any students interested in farming or research in related fields, this site is a good place to start. Their "Education and Outreach" page offers plenty of free resources for students, teachers, and parents.

Vocational Information Center—Computer Science Career Guide

www.khake.com/page17.html

Here is a seemingly infinite list of careers and jobs in computer science and information technology. Job descriptions are included, along with companion information such as duties, skills, salaries, and training requirements.

In the next chapter, we chat with some professionals who share their experiences in and recommendations for exposing students to STEM curriculum and careers.

Chapter 3

Interviews with
STEM Professionals

THE SUCCESS OF CAREER AWARENESS programs for K–12 students depends in large part on the success of building relationships with professionals in the STEM fields. By tapping children's natural curiosity about the world and about the adults who inhabit that world, by taking advantage of no-cost or low-cost digital communications technologies, we can guide students toward productive futures long before they graduate from the secondary school classroom.

This chapter consists of several interviews with professionals in STEM fields who share their stories, their recommendations, and their opinions on the future of STEM education.

INTERVIEW

Patricia Galloway

Patricia D. Galloway, PE, CPENG, PMP, MRICS, CFCC, is the chief executive officer of Pegasus Global Holdings and is the vice chair of the National Science Board.

I first ran across Patricia Galloway's name when I was reading a report coproduced by the National Science Board. Because I was looking for women in the STEM fields who had made a difference, I decided to investigate. I discovered that Galloway is a civil engineer and not only has had an impressive career, but also has taken time to share her own inspiration and insights with K–12 classroom students. She has also written a book, *The 21st Century Engineer—A Blueprint for Engineering Education Reform*, published by ASCE Press.

She is quoted on Engineer Girl, a career-based website sponsored by the National Academy of Engineering (www.engineergirl.org): "Becoming the first woman president of the American Society of Civil Engineers in 152 years was truly the most awesome achievement, of which I am very proud." She also shared some of the best parts of being an engineer—that she can be creative and make dreams come true. She told youngsters who might be considering a career like hers, young girls in particular, not to ever let anyone tell them it couldn't be done.

Camille: What skills for a global economy, in your estimation, do students need that they may not be getting in K–12 classrooms?

Patricia: Math, science, pre-engineering … what it is, why is engineering is important to our lives. Also, K–12 kids need a general understanding of economics and geography—what GDP is, how the world operates; about cultures and history as it shapes our future in both politics and world economy.

Camille: I know you've been an active partner with K–12 education. In what ways do you suggest working professionals reach out to K–12 students to introduce and interest them in STEM careers?

Patricia: By going to the classroom and getting involved in an activity that works with the kids so they can see what it is all about. Talking heads is no longer a good method and can actually turn kids against wanting to do STEM careers.

[Kids need] after-school projects and community activity related to STEM, such as building, or projects for the needy, Girl Scouts, and activities that go toward earning badges in STEM areas. Books and videos that have interesting and fun stories about STEM with characters so that briefings can be shared. Real-life examples of engineering projects and why the project is of value to society. Nearly every type of engineering can be incorporated into nearly every subject area discussed in K–12 education.

Art was the love of my life, and I won several awards for my pencil sketches. I was sure I was going to be either an interpreter for the United Nations or a lawyer! Then I attended a mandatory lecture at my high school about engineering. The professor, from the University of Kentucky, was a structural civil engineer and had brought along several renderings of buildings. These renderings caught my eye because one of the items that I sketched the most was buildings. The professor added that, as a woman, I would have wonderful opportunities in the engineering field and would command a nice salary. I was sold!

Camille: Do you believe educators are taking seriously the call, the need for students to take an interest in math and science?

Patricia: No. Unless the teacher is someone with this skill background, I foresee there is a fear factor of not knowing and because they don't know, they do not share.

Camille: I ran across a recent study citing a lack of retention of qualified people entering STEM fields. Could the reason be that futures in STEM fields are not seen as attractive?

Patricia: Absolutely! Search Google for "extraordinary women engineers project" and click on the report funded by NSF that researched why girls between 14 and 17 years of age were not interested in becoming engineers. You'll find that the people who influence what career paths girls might follow do not understand what a career in engineering looks like or believe that it's a likely career choice for girls. It's not an issue of ability.

Camille: I know you've been active as a mentor for young women. In what ways do you believe you have served as a role model for girls thinking about entering engineering fields?

Patricia: My long-term professional goals are to, one, serve as a role model that young women can look up to and two, write books. I have already written my first book, *The 21st Century Engineer*, which is about the skill sets an engineer needs to survive in the 21st century. I'd like to write another book that will describe what I believe it takes to succeed as a woman in the engineering and construction industries. The other book will be about Emily Roebling and her role in building the Brooklyn Bridge and will be based on the play that I produced and have acted; it's called *So Mrs. Roebling—What's Your Side of the Story?*

Becoming the first woman president of the American Society of Civil Engineers in 152 years was truly the most awesome achievement, of which I am very proud. Having achieved this accomplishment allowed me to pave the way and shatter that glass ceiling, serving as a role model to both young girls and women to be whatever they want to be and knowing they can achieve anything they desire to do. I am also honored that I was appointed to the National Science Board, one of 24 people appointed by the president to be involved with some of the nation's most amazing science and engineering research projects, which will continue to make our world a better place to be.

Camille: What advice would you give to a young woman considering a career in engineering?

Patricia: Remember the 4 C's: Communication, Confidence, Commitment, and Credentials. To be successful, it is extremely important to be able to communicate effectively with everyone, not just your technical peers. Communication includes writing, talking, and listening. Having the confidence in yourself is equally as important, as it provides assurance to your peers, your employer, and your clients that you can and will deliver what you say you can and will do. Both communication and confidence are base premises to commitment. Once you tell someone you will do something, you must follow through. Once you fail to do so, doubt will always exist in the other person's mind and your potential opportunities may be passed on to someone else. Finally, you are never too old to stop learning. It's a lifelong process. Advanced degrees, researching and writing papers, and studying to obtain licenses and certifications—such as a Professional Engineer's license and a Project Management Certification—will be a key to getting your foot into the door. The rest will be up to how you handle yourself and what you know about your subject. Homework never goes away, and understanding the subject more than your client will always work in your favor!

Camille: That is truly great advice. Are there any other stories or comments you would like to share?

Patricia: I am proud to be an engineer. We live in an opportune time to make a difference in the world and to really make the world a better place to live in, both for people and for the environment. We need solutions to world problems that require engineering skills, creative minds, and energetic teams. Now is the time to want to be an engineer. And remember, never let anyone tell you it can't be done.

INTERVIEW

Laurence Peters

Laurence Peters was born in London, England. He studied at the University of Sussex, where he received a BA degree in English literature in 1974. He received his MA (Education) degree in the theory and practice of English teaching from the University of London, Institute of Education (1978), and a PhD from the University of Michigan. After writing and teaching, he gained a law degree from the University of Maryland in 1986 and became counsel to the Subcommittee on Select Education and Civil Rights for the U.S. House of Representatives (1986–1993) before serving as a senior policy advisor to the U.S. Department of Education (1993–2001).

Subsequently Peters directed the Mid-Atlantic Regional Technology in Education Consortium (MAR*TEC) working with five states (Pennsylvania, Maryland, Delaware, Washington DC, and New Jersey) to assist their efforts to integrate technology into the curriculum. He currently serves as an educational technology consultant and vice president of the National Education Foundation. He is the author of *Global Education*.

I have worked with Laurence on his global classrooms projects and know him to be well versed in connecting classrooms with global awareness resources, projects, and partners. I know him to be passionate in this arena. When I asked him to contribute to the conversation for this book, he readily accepted.

Camille: Do you believe educators are taking seriously the need for students to take an interest in science and math?

Laurence: In many ways they are not. If we look back to 1960, one out of every six—17%—of U.S. bachelor or graduate degrees was awarded in engineering, mathematics, or the physical sciences. Despite the fuss about Sputnik and the Cold War, by 2001 that number dropped to less than 1 in 10, just 8% of all degrees. So our reaction, in essence, was to strengthen math and science requirements. Students had to take more credit hours in math and science classes to graduate.

This sounds good, but it does not in any fundamental way change the nature of the problem. And this is despite the fact that a number of reports and experts have called for more hands-on teaching of science and less textbook approaches. The curriculum is still not well designed, particularly in the middle and high school years, to motivate students to learn math and science. Interest generally among the public and young people has exploded—we now have the Discovery Channel and many others like it devoted to high-quality science programming. We even have stores and museums that house exciting displays of science-related materials.

We need to dramatically rethink our approaches. Why not build a curriculum around students' interests? These days it would include robots, video games, technology, computers—and then work backwards so that students realize that in order to really have fun with them—to build and play with them at more advanced levels—they need to understand math and science. We don't have to spend so much time teaching to kids when they already have so much natural curiosity about the world. But teachers can't do this singlehandedly. The dismal numbers of students who enter math and science should be a worry signal to our policy makers that all is not well and that we can't afford to continue to window-dress the issue.

Camille: In your opinion, what skills will be required to ensure innovation in the future?

Laurence: The people in our society who are the best at innovation are not always our academic high fliers—they are very often students who have a natural curiosity about the world as well as an ability to think both creatively and divergently about problems. Many would argue that such skills cannot be taught—they are somehow hardwired and so people like Bill Gates are exceptional geniuses that occur once or twice in a generation. Malcolm Gladwell's stimulating book, *Outliers*, has a different take on this, however—he takes a closer look at a few exceptional individuals like Gates and Bill Joy, the founder of Sun Microsystems—that their environment, in both cases their good fortune in being exposed at a critical time in their development to very powerful computers, allowed them to channel their intellectual passions into work they enjoyed. So if schools want to cultivate more innovators, they have to give their students more room and freedom to try and fail at more things and not do it for the extrinsic rewards—letter grades—but for the intrinsic rewards, the pleasure and satisfaction at succeeding at difficult tasks.

Camille: We've heard the phrase "21st-century skills" for a long time. In your opinion, in what ways has the definition of 21st-century skills changed over the past 20 years?

Laurence: I think there is a more serious recognition concerning the need to think about what key role math, science, engineering, and technology—STEM skills—will play in the 21st century. There is also a stronger focus on the role of problem solving and teamwork skills to communicate globally using technology. We also have been recently reminding ourselves about the need for two things to be successful in the 21st century: knowledge of how to learn and how to be a critical and empowered member of a community of learners, whether it is in a workplace community or as a member of society more broadly.

Camille: What stands in the way of schools making use of the "participatory Internet"?

Laurence: In one word: firewalls. There are physical firewalls that schools impose concerning their own legal vulnerabilities, as *in loco parentis* for students who might be subject to online predators. And there are metaphorical firewalls that prevent some school leaders from thinking creatively about the use of the Internet for all kinds of subject areas.

In the area of the lack of imagination concerning the participatory Internet—the metaphorical firewalls—higher education in particular and superintendents need to inform themselves of the highly creative ways that a wide variety of Web 2.0 tools can assist student learning. We have not invested nearly enough in the necessary research for this to take place, but we can make a start and need to do this soon, if only to banish some of the fear about the new technologies.

Camille: Do you believe that students are being alienated from school because of a lack of relevance in the way teachers teach and the ways they are being asked to learn?

Laurence: In a word, yes. The key is to provide students with more choice in what and how they learn. We tend to confuse two things in education too easily. One is the content we have to learn because society agrees that an educated individual needs to know certain things about the world, which is typically defined in terms of the curriculum and assessments we ask states to develop and schools to become accountable for. The second area is a disposition to learn and to enjoy learning so much that it is easy to see oneself as a lifelong learner. If we focus too much on the content at the expense of the process of becoming a learner, then we produce either dolts—people who can recite information and regurgitate facts when asked but cannot think creatively as well as critically—or people who reject formal schooling altogether and become dropouts.

Reading a book like *Reading Don't Fix No Chevys* reminds you about the way that you can gain far more participation and add relevance to the curriculum if you don't prescribe everything—if teachers allow students to reach general curriculum goals through means that interest them. You as a teacher guide them, of course, by the questions you ask and the interest you show in responding to their answers and their progress. So authors Smith and Wilhelm show this beautifully in their study of male adolescent readers—it was not that these young men did not read, it was that they read differently from the way that schools wanted them to read; that was the issue that the researchers uncovered. Many were voracious readers of things like car manuals—the role of the teacher is to guide them so they don't just read car manuals and they get interested in heroes who they can identify with who share their values, not necessarily the school's values.

One lesson I draw from this is that if you ignore student tastes and interests and insist they share yours, there is only a limited possibility for growth. If you acknowledge tastes and interests, you can meet them somewhere in the middle and help them see how their interest in cars, for example, might be connected to the schools' more formal concerns—that they also know science, engineering, and math as well as history, geography, social studies, and language arts. All of these subjects can be linked creatively together if you first acknowledge your learner's interests and then empower your learner to navigate a path forward. Technology, because it allows for so much independent learning, should be our friend in this endeavor, and we need to embrace it, therefore, far more than we do in schools to help achieve these ends.

INTERVIEW

Lynne Schrum

Lynne Schrum is a professor and coordinator of elementary education in the College of Education and Human Development at George Mason University. Her research and teaching focus on appropriate uses of information technology, online and distance learning, and preparing teachers for the 21st century. She has written five books and numerous articles on these subjects; the most recent two are *Web 2.0 How-To for Educators*, and *Leading a 21st Century School: Harnessing Technology for Engagement and Achievement*. Lynne was recently on AERA's council, is editor of the *Journal of Research on Technology in Education* (JRTE) (2002–2011), and is a past president of the International Society for Technology in Education (ISTE). More information can be found at http://mason.gmu.edu/~lschrum.

I've known Lynne as a colleague in the educational technology field for more than 20 years. As I spoke with her, I was reminded that there are often assumptions about teachers, as well as how important it is to look at and to understand the big picture. She also reaffirmed what I've thought quietly for a long time: without strong leadership, you can't blame teachers in the classroom for the slow change process.

Camille: The word *technology* is vague. It covers a lot of territory. There is a need for kids to be prepared for STEM careers, but it's more than just technology: it's understanding the larger world, the change that's going on in the world, the global economy kids will one day be part of—they're going to need to be well versed in technologies that are now often blocked in schools. Many of them are going to need to know about social networking, and not in the pop-culture way we think of it. That's how businesses are going to be run and how science is going to organize research. We're talking about a worldwide shift.

Lynne: We are doing them a disservice if we don't even broach the topic with them or encourage them. The kids have no fears. I've been looking at immersive games (multiuser virtual environments—MUVEs)—the whole idea of Quest Atlantis, and River City, using interactive media to learn. These are the kinds of things that would encourage kids to do all kinds of things that let them see and participate in the world in a larger sense. We don't do much to take advantage of the possibilities.

Camille: They are fearless and they do know how to use that technology, but they may not know how to use it intelligently; and they may not understand the effects and the safety issues. If teachers are behind the pack and can't guide them through the ethical and safety issues, then they are doing the students a disservice.

Lynne: I totally agree with you. Again, I tend very much to not put blame on anyone or any part of the puzzle because I don't think it's helpful and there's enough of that to go around. You've mentioned some of this: we block technology at the door and we don't provide enough professional development and on and on and on. But it's also going to take new research that demonstrates what the power is, and so far we haven't had a lot of great research. We're starting to see more. We need to be able to say demonstrably, "If we can start using these, kids are going to be able to do X, Y, and Z." That's what we want to know, what's the bottom line? What's the payoff? Not with test scores so much, but what skills will they have, what knowledge will they have? How are they going to face the world? What are they going to think about?

Camille: Would it be fair to say that if we wait for the science, in our lifetimes, our career lifetime, we won't see the kind of change we were calling for in 1983, '89, '91—when some of the big reform cries came out?

Lynne: I agree with you. I don't think we can wait. We have to do it simultaneously. We have to fund good research—make the research more accessible. With most of the professional development for administrators, there's very little about technology, at least in terms of change—what's possible, what could be done, how it could be done. So again, we've got people we're asking to do things on a leap of faith, that this is good for you. So we have to do it all at the same time.

Camille: I'm interested in hearing your thoughts about the disconnect between the need for preparation for STEM careers and what's actually happening in the classroom—especially for young girls.

Lynne: I'm very happy to talk about that. It's near and dear to my heart. Things are better now, but I wish there were some easy answers. There are some examples of good things—an engineering program that goes into the elementary school and helps kids start to see the power—see that it's not just geeky stuff; it's really fun, engaging activities for kids in the STEM areas. We've seen some good, but it's not systematized.

There are some funding streams that try to promote STEM careers, but they aren't widely implemented in schools, so some people get it and some people don't. I think it has a lot to do with where you are, where you go to school, how much money your school district has for extra things—they would call it "extra." It's not that we don't know how to do this; it's just that it's not happening everywhere. We're starting to see more encouragement from the National Science Foundation (NSF)—they had some grants to encourage STEM projects and careers.

We don't have enough STEM teachers. We don't have enough teachers that are interested and can serve as role models. That's particularly true for young girls. Research suggests if young girls don't see role models, then they see that as a boy's thing only—so we've got to fight that. If you look at what we know about young women in schools, as they approach puberty, interest in STEM areas declines. Some businesses have done some mentoring with middle school girls and all kinds of things to try and encourage them. There's some evidence in the literature that girls in single-sex STEM classes do much better because they are not embarrassed to answer questions about science, math, engineering. But of course, that's against some of the rules. My belief is that we have to start young. We have to get small children to understand about science, and there I will tell you that I do not believe we do a very good job with our elementary teachers, getting them ready to do that. A lot of them don't like science, they don't know about science so they stay away from it—they don't want to teach it, all those things. And that to me is a real tragedy.

Camille: Would you say that leadership is as important a skill as being a technician?

Lynne: To me, it's the missing link. We don't talk about it very much and we have to. I believe that we've got to put energy around knowing what to do in the change process. Change is hard. These people who are going to be leading our schools have to know how to do that. I don't think right now we're doing a very good job of getting them ready to do that. All the books on effective leadership won't make a difference if the potential leaders don't see the need to read them.

INTERVIEW

Michael Clark

Michael Clark studied chemistry at the College of Forestry at Syracuse University. Later, he joined the U.S. Air Force, where he was selected to attend Special Electronics training. He was posted to a job monitoring the Earth's ionosphere and near space environment for clandestine high-altitude nuclear explosions using very low frequency phase anomaly, atmospheric fluorescence, and infrasound techniques. He also monitored the Earth's oceans for underwater explosions using the hydroacoustic technique. He also served as a television studio engineer, doing television camera setup, electronics maintenance, and videotape operations for training productions. Michael accepted a position with Science Applications International Corporation (SAIC) in Arlington, Virginia, as a global data analyst and analysis operations technique developer for the Group of Scientific Experts Technical Test 3 (GSETT3). This was a prelude to start-up operations of the Prototype International Data Center (PIDC). PIDC was the successful forerunner of the International Data Centre (IDC) of the Comprehensive Test Ban Treaty Organization (CTBTO) in Vienna. In 1998, he accepted a position as lead analyst and analysis unit head for the CTBTO IDC in Vienna, Austria, where he worked until his retirement in 2007. He works now as an independent data analyst and consultant in northern Virginia.

I went to high school with Michael Clark. I knew from personal experience that he had access, during his high school experience, to some of the best science and math teachers New York state had to offer. I knew that he went on to excel in a career in a STEM field and decided to ask him if he'd be willing to reflect on his career for the purpose of this book.

Camille: What skills for the emerging global economy are students not getting in today's primary and secondary school classrooms?

Michael: In my opinion, one of the best skills a student should have is how to take advantage of experience. I've been away from the K–12 classroom for a long time but have instructed students right out of high school. Many of them are highly motivated to learn but have difficulty relating relatively arcane work practices to the academia they have been immersed in for most of their life. A good dose of hands-on experience toward a goal of excellence in the workplace is great skill development.

Camille: Tell me a little bit about your career and the significant events that led you to that career.

Michael: Perhaps the most significant event that led me to my career, which culminated, you might say, in my becoming a data analyst and trainer for the Comprehensive Test Ban Treaty, occurred way back in high school when I realized that I had a fascination with science classes, and that chemistry and physics were at the top of the list. I can remember sitting in both Mrs. Baner's chemistry class, and Mr. Fetterman's physics and advanced chemistry class, and knowing the answers to questions almost before they finished asking them. Later on, I was hand-picked for very specialized training, I was able to excel in a highly technical field. Later on, I was able to teach others the how-tos of the system and proudly watch them excel. So one success led to the next and held my interest.

Camille: So now that you've experienced more than two decades of high-level work in the technology and science fields, in your opinion, what skills will be required to ensure innovation in the future? The U.S. has been an innovative society, but now I'm reading that it's not a given that the U.S. will maintain its position as a world leader in innovation.

Michael: In my opinion, much of innovation comes from being able to relate to the past and present, and bouncing one fact or technique off one's native curiosity with a view toward the impossible. Keeping a sense of youth and fun and games tends to drive the impossible back into the caves. There's a lot to be said about the adage, "Sorry, I didn't know it couldn't be done, so I just went ahead and did it." I actually had that happen to me once, doing something "impossible" but useful with a piece of antiquated equipment just by playing with it.

Camille: So you're saying give kids the freedom to be creative and follow their curiosity is the best insurance to retain a culture of innovation?

Michael: Cultured curiosity and creativity in a free environment goes a long way. A leadership model and mentor is also important to young minds, especially those who have difficulty staying focused. A good role model coupled with a can-do leadership style that shows success in the STEM fields will culture innovation possibly better than anything else. Leadership is tricky, though—young people can turn off if they feel coerced, or lectured.

Camille: Mike, in your experience, what are some of the ways working professionals can reach out to K–12 students to inspire them and interest them in STEM careers?

Michael: That can be a tough one. I have to say that working professionals need to remember their roots and relate to others following their paths. I have seen too many professionals sit on their PhDs and actually believe they are the top dog in their professions while knocking back others' ideas as undesired rivals. That kind of "Not-Invented-Here" arrogant attitude is definitely not motivational to K–12 students.

Camille: So what first inspired you to be a scientist? Did you know back when we were in high school?

Michael: As I said earlier, I seemed to have had an aptitude for the sciences from a young age. Growing up in the '50s and '60s, we had a lot of environmental science all around, from supersonic aircraft to the space program. We were awash in science, and I guess I naturally followed.

Camille: Do you believe educators are taking seriously the call for students to take an interest in science, technology, and math?

Michael: From what I see, educators are exceedingly serious about these subjects because they teach them, and some of the great teachers are great because they are inspirational to their students. Science, math, and technology rub off on the K–12 crowd if they get inspired. One problem many teachers seem to develop, though, is not relating their subjects to the students' real world. It's very easy to get complacent, following canned lesson plans. A challenge educators need to keep in focus is how to bring the current interests of their students—cell phones, iPods, etc.—into the realm of academia. How does that music get into the iPod, anyway? Never authoritatively tell a student that something is impossible or stupid. While that may be a challenge for some, it can be a total turn-off for some with still-developing confidence and motivation in the sciences.

Camille: What about critical-thinking and problem-solving skills—do you think these skills are more important for young students to learn today than 30 years ago?

Michael: Critical-thinking and problem-solving skills are probably just as important today as 30 years ago, and are probably much the same. It's just that the problems have changed. The thinking processes and skills are adapted to solving the problems whatever they are. They relate to human curiosity, which I believe can solve just about anything, given time.

Camille: What is the connection between education and economic innovation and competitiveness?

Michael: Education brings the toolsets to the innovator and competitor to use. It unlocks the methods for the mind to jump that one-step-ahead of one's peers, and succeed. Education is not degrees or adding letters behind one's name, but understanding how things are fundamentally. There are a lot of examples of degree-less people who had the drive to apply what they knew and innovated into exceptionally competitive businesses.

Camille: In what ways—you may have noticed during your own work—are the technological demands of the workforce increasing?

Michael: The biggest increases in technological demands are related to the ever-increasing speed of modern living. Just about the time you assimilate the concept of an issue, a new innovation drops out of the sky and turns the known world upside down. Computers are a good example, with PCs or cell phones becoming obsolete between the time you buy them and when you get them home. The acceleration of rate of exposure to new concepts gives less and less time to assimilate the basic concepts, and people are getting left behind. No one can take it all in, and the threads to ideas outside our ever-sharpening focus can get cut, resulting in fewer linkages that might result in new innovations.

Camille: There is a recent study that cites a lack of retention of qualified people entering STEM fields out of college. Could the reason be that futures in STEM fields are not attractive?

Michael: One serious problem is a perceived lack of glamour of basic science. Many qualified science majors are lured away to fields with more individualized recognition. And the recognition often translates into better promotion. There's a perception that work in basic science is akin to day-labor, where someone else profits from the work. Also, starting at the bottom and working one's way up seems old-fashioned and counterproductive to some. Management needs to keep their focus on their support base and the people who get their hands dirty, so to speak, and provide recognition and advancement to keep qualified people—a basic function of leadership that often gets overlooked.

Camille: What does the workplace of the future look like to you?

Michael: The workplace of the future is here now. It's constantly evolving and morphing into something that it wasn't just yesterday. A critical part of the workplace is the human aspect. Technology is great, but if it puts people somewhere they don't want to be, then it's not going to be nearly as useful as it could be. Technology is going to grow at ever-increasing rates and needs to be marketed in human terms to be truly useful.

Camille: We hear a lot about 21st-century skills. How would you define, based on your work experiences, these so-called 21st-century skills?

Michael: Twenty-first-century skills are a function of what needs to be accomplished and what's interesting to the individual. The successful individual will always develop the new skills necessary to advance. Nineteenth- and 20th-century skills are still needed as a basis to develop those yet-unknown 21st-century skills and as a reality check to keep expectations in line. You have to be careful not to block or belittle dreams—because dreams are where most real innovation originates, and dreams guide people's interests and development of skills.

Camille: Do you believe the new "participatory Internet" will affect professionalism in science and engineering?

Michael: The participatory Internet will improve professionalism in science and engineering in some ways, but it could also result in some detriments if egos get in the way. Advances will continue to come from idea seeding, sharing, and collaboration, which I think is great. This sharing is one definition of professionalism. Human nature, you know, gets in the way—competition and people with less-than-ideal integrity who don't attribute properly, and that slows down real progress.

Chapter 4

It Takes a Village: Partnerships for Learning

To be most successful at improving the global workforce and producing better citizens, we must create alignment and develop meaningful partnerships.

—CHARLES MITCHELL

"IT TAKES A VILLAGE to raise a child." The 1990s catchphrase can represent the importance of education in our society and the role that communities play in developing strong schools. Today, most businesses and organizations contribute to K–12 schools in some way. They may give direct donations; they may provide contributions of products, or capital funding. Some provide their employees for teacher training or career awareness programs. Many companies contribute expertise in many ways through all types of partnerships.

From medical institutions to manufacturing companies to communications and media companies, all of commerce and industry around the globe depend on an emerging workforce ready to fill a wide range of jobs, schooled in how to adapt to ever-changing technologies in a knowledge-based society. More than ever, business, industry, the arts, and communications corporations and organizations are ready to partner with schools in their communities and across the nation to help teachers and students keep in touch with what's going on, locally and globally.

This chapter provides strategies to lay the groundwork for career awareness partnerships for learning as well as two examples of excellent existing partnership programs. My goal is to help educators locate and approach educational, scientific, health care, and technology-based groups in search of classroom partnerships from which to build a community of learning around career readiness for K–12 students.

Partnerships with professionals and their organizations are supported by the application of an explosion of production, communication, and collaboration technologies. Videoconferencing brings real-life professionals into the classroom, allowing students to interact face-to-face with role models, ask questions, and get to know through their own firsthand investigation what it's like to be a scientist in the global warming field, for example, and what it took to become one. Videoconferencing also supports virtual field trips for students to hundreds of sciences centers and museums all over the world. Locally, many businesses now have videoconferencing in place, and savvy teachers can establish mentorship programs using videoconferencing. This is especially rewarding for rural schools that would ordinarily never have this kind of access. Videoconferencing also opens doors for partnerships with extremely busy professionals who don't have time to travel to classrooms. It helps build authentic relationships in ways that email or desktop communications cannot.

Web-based tools such as webcasts, podcasts, videocasts, blogs, video streaming, social media, and even email also provide tools to create and sustain partnerships. Experts and mentors can communicate with students in classrooms by creating on-demand presentations. Students can inform community partners about their progress using safe student blogs and wikis.

Partnership-Building Strategies: Getting Started

Schools can make use of community partnerships to help prepare students for careers in STEM fields. How can they effectively establish and sustain these partnerships without cutting into teachers' already overflowing workloads? One of the keys to developing effective partnerships is to know what and who is out there, where to access these resources, how to approach the right person, and how to understand what the organization or person may have to offer.

I suggest schools consider starting partnership building by simply building relationships with parents of students. Find out who they are, what they may have to offer, and what level of interest they have in contributing. Students and their teachers can create classroom Nings (social networking sites) to explore the careers and occupations of parents and other community members. Almost all parents—and many community members—will usually want to contribute. Web 2.0 technologies make partnerships possible for busy parents and community partners.

Another key is to know how to fit the resource or opportunity into the curriculum and how to communicate needs and requests. One of the elements of good partnering is good communication. Keep track of whom you've talked to, what you've researched, and the ways volunteers might interface with classrooms or your school. Track the history of the partnership. In what ways has the individual or organization interfaced with classrooms? What was the outcome, and what will be the follow-up, if any?

You'll find a sample template for tracking partnerships at the end of this chapter (see page 54). I suggest using an online spreadsheet or a database, though you can use paper, if you must, but keep good records of all encounters and any required follow-up including thank-you notes. Though this may sound obvious, extending a thank-you in writing is important and often forgotten. Business contributors generally appreciate a three-month follow-up: How is it going? What has been accomplished? Sometimes it's appropriate to thank a partner by publishing a newsletter article. Many teachers and their students are using wikis to publish classroom newsletters. You can also include a newsletter feature on your parent partnership Ning, or other customized social networking tool.

If the partnership or the project is significant, talk to your district's public relations director about sending out a press release. Most businesses like the recognition. For a large project, it's appropriate to ask your contacts what they want, or what their policy is regarding publicity.

The sample Partnership Development form at the end of this chapter is simply an example of the kind of information you might want to track, whatever tool you might use, as you make contact with potential partners. The idea is to track your partnership development, activities, and contacts. Use the information year after year and build on the partnerships over time.

Also at the end of the chapter, you will find the Digital Partnerships form, which is designed to help prepare for, implement, and follow up on career development partnerships. These might include interactive videoconference guest speakers, virtual field-trip presenters, and workshops with career mentors.

STEM Partnerships Up Close

The Wisconsin Department of Public Instruction (2006), in its report "State Superintendent's High School Task Force," says,

> Helping students see the need for education takes a community approach. Schools must be "of the community"—both a resource for community events and a beneficiary of community resources that provide students with opportunities to learn. The leadership of business representatives is especially important to help ensure that learning is relevant and will adequately prepare students for post-high school plans. (p. 22)

Following are examples of successful, established STEM career classroom partnerships.

Project Lead the Way

Project Lead the Way (PLTW; www.pltw.com), a national initiative to provide K–12 students with career and college-readiness opportunities in STEM fields, has taken hold in schools around the United States. The idea behind the program is: How can we get more students interested in careers in science, technology, engineering, and math? PLTW provides a challenging curriculum tailored for specific grades that can be integrated into regular class schedules.

Local programs are supported by networks of volunteers and supporters—similar to the first NetDay initiative to wire schools around the United States in 1997. Local partners contribute as mentors, or by giving cash or product donations.

On a national level, the program is supported by large donations of cash and technology by corporate partners in the engineering and biomedical industries. Companies such as Autodesk, EdgeCam, and Fischertechnik provide software packages for PLTW courses. They also offer grant programs, training in curriculum development, and even a social networking site for students interested in these career paths.

Launched in 1997, this partnership program of rigorous curriculum, training, and networking resources for middle and high school students has been implemented in more than 3,000 middle and high schools in every state.

Project leaders have reported that participating students, based on postproject surveys, are as much as 10 times more likely to elect science or engineering courses of study in college and twice as likely to graduate in that field.

DIGITS

Fifty partner companies, including iRobot and Google, helped launch DIGITS (www.digits.us.com), a Massachusetts initiative to dispatch scientists and engineers to sixth grade classrooms around the state. Founders of DIGITS chose sixth graders based on a belief that by seventh grade, kids are already forming negative attitudes about careers in science and math. Joyce Plotkin, chair of the STEMTech Alliance and president emerita of the Massachusetts Technology Leadership Council says,

> A strong partnership among technology associations, industry professionals, government and schools is the best way to stimulate student interest in math and science education. As a result of the partnership we created in Massachusetts, we were able to develop an exciting new program that will engage students and open their minds to the possibilities of STEM careers. Also, we are pleased that this program will help to lay the groundwork for continued science and technology leadership in the Commonwealth. (Business Wire, 2009)

The idea is to boost student interest in math and science careers. The initiative is supported by a coalition of six statewide science and technology association partners. They are funded by their Department of Higher Education's STEM Pipeline Fund.

DIGITS is designed to show students what sort of careers are available if they study STEM subjects. Volunteer partners, or "ambassadors," tell students about their own jobs, the industry they work in, and how their education helped lead them to their STEM career.

OMSI

There are an abundance of regional science centers throughout the United States and throughout the world. In the past, these centers were generally museums that also offered a variety of student programs and various traveling exhibits and permanent installations. Sadly, if your school is not located within a couple of hours' ride from the science center, it's not likely your students would ever get to visit these rich educational resources, unless they were lucky enough to go with their parents during a vacation. With distance learning technologies, and now digital media technologies, students and teachers have easy access to science centers once their networks, hardware, and innovative educators are in place. The final step is establishing the partnership between your school or classroom and the science center, or simply knowing where to look on the Internet to find access to their programs.

In my state, Oregon, we are lucky to have the Oregon Museum of Science and Industry in Portland, fondly known by Oregonians as OMSI. About 90% of the geographic area of the state does not have easy physical access to OMSI.

As the distance learning coordinator at the Oregon Department of Education for many years, it was my pleasure to oversee the deployment and implementation of the state's educational videoconferencing and distance learning network. This network, once in place, allowed teachers to attend all kinds of professional development programs in Portland, Salem, Eugene, and Medford that before would have taken at least two days of travel time for educators from the eastern part of the state. Educators in Medford, located almost at the California border, at one time had to travel more than three hours one way just to attend a one-hour meeting or a half-day training session. Although accessing professional development from a distance isn't always the best solution, as a supplement for face-to-face programs, or as an alternative to none at all, it is an extraordinary opportunity.

OMSI was the first content provider in Oregon to implement distance learning in order to reach out to the statewide constituency of educators and students. The state department of education donated two room-sized videoconference units that were no longer working. Though these were thought to be throwaways by the telephone company tech staff, OMSI tech staff were able, in less than a day's time, to pick up the two units and merge them into a working videoconference system. In no time, they were offering professional development services in science education to teachers in all corners of the state. In partnership with education service districts and the department of education, they brought special events to an emerging statewide community of learning—an afternoon meeting with Don Pettit, a local hero and one of the International Space Station astronauts, for example. Students around the state asked him questions about how he became an astronaut and about bathroom issues. No longer was the idea of being a national hero and scientist something out of their reach or beyond their grasp.

In less than a decade, OMSI has become a nationally recognized content provider for both students and educators. Using videoconferencing and other digital media tools, they have:

- Established a working partnership with the libraries of Eastern Oregon

- Created distance-learning programs to deliver NASA-linked science curriculum and professional development in nine rural Oregon regions

- Created a region-wide network of teachers and public librarians as mentors and "ambassadors"

- Extended a technology infrastructure, providing access for Oregon's rural K–12 schools and communities

- Provided museum-based and traveling outreach programs to augment educational science programs

Their digital distance learning program has now put OMSI within reach of educators and students all over the state, and beyond. They say they have delivered 150 science outreach programs to 3,500 students in remote and underserved rural regions throughout the state. These programs included The JASON Expedition, Disappearing Wetlands, and The Science of Lewis & Clark.

One particular goal of OMSI was to increase the comfort level for teachers in using technology in science education and to increase student interest in STEM careers. Final project reports indicate that there was a 67% increase in the use of technology in science education by participating teachers, and 70% of teachers reported that their students had increased their interest in science, technology, engineering, and mathematics careers. Of the teachers surveyed after the completion of the OMSI professional development projects, 80% wanted to increase their students' interest in STEM careers.

OMSI's digital labs, over the reporting period, received 18,996 visits, close to 50% of the total number of licensed staff in Oregon's public schools.

Marilyn Johnson, director of research and development in education at OMSI, gave me her opinion about the role of the regional science center in education:

> Regional science centers like OMSI can form a vital component of STEM education because science center educators are experts in attracting and engaging audiences—children, teachers, parents, and the general public. While teachers know how to deepen students' understanding of these subjects, they are often limited in their ability to provide excitement or address the breadth of interest among their students. So science centers provide an array of "wow" experiences that motivate students to learn, to delve deeper. They make things explode … they explore tide pools, or they take you on a tour of the universe in a planetarium. And these landmark experiences provide unforgettable hooks to benchmarks in STEM formal education. Science centers also extend the breadth of resources and content expertise such as curricular enhancements, web interactivities, podcasts, virtual field trips, and interactive videoconferencing both for students and teachers.
>
> OMSI has been able, through a combination of virtual and face-to-face, to support a regional community that encompasses a five-state region. Many remote rural communities are able to fully participate in unique and personalized OMSI programs such as The Physics of Music. This has been an amazing success, and through programs like these we hope to level the STEM playing field between communities that are resource-rich and those with limited resources.

Doug Buchanan, marketing manager with the Education Department at the Center of Science and Industry (COSI) in Columbus, Ohio, also spoke to me on this topic:

> COSI's mission is to actively seek to empower teachers to expose students to real science and real scientists through our videoconference programs. Our goal is to encourage students to embrace science as part of everyday life, to use science to think critically about issues, to make informed decisions, and to solve challenges. COSI inspires an excitement for science

and learning and we hope the outcome is to influence and inspire innovation. Just maybe, because of interaction with our organization, students will pursue science educational opportunities throughout their lives.

ECORS

The case study presented in Chapter 5, "Extending Career Options for Rural Students" (ECORS), demonstrates how 17 schools in Oregon collaborated to integrate videoconferencing to make career awareness opportunities available to their rural student population. Many of these students were losing interest in school and were dropping out at alarming rates. Integrating technology into the classroom, connecting students with people beyond their borders, helped these students begin to understand why they were in school, and they became engaged in their learning.

Keys to Successful Partnerships

The common denominator of community partners, be they big corporations or individuals, is the desire to be acknowledged. Try to be sensitive to what kind of acknowledgment your partner wants—a write-up in the paper or a quiet thank-you note. Once you've thanked your classroom partners, don't forget them after they walk out the door; keep them informed about the progress of your project if you want to maintain the relationship. If you have access to wikis or blogs, these tools provide an efficient format for keeping classroom partners and the community informed over time about your success and your progress. A regular newsletter filled with news and achievements will put your school and classrooms on the radar screen of those who have helped out in the past.

Accountability is a key for success. Follow up and follow through. I recommend that you create templates similar to those shown in Figures 4.1 and 4.2. In the end, be sure to share the credit and provide recognition when it is appropriate. Education and its impact on the workforce of the future are evolving into a major issue for companies (Barrington & Mitchell, 2008). If you as an educator are successful at partnership development, your students will benefit for years to come.

PARTNERSHIP DEVELOPMENT	
Name of Organization	Location
Contact Person	Date of First Contact
Phone / Email	Web
Partnership Goals	Partnership Ideas
Areas of Expertise	Curriculum Tie-ins/Topic
Communications/Technology Tools	Materials/Multimedia Required
Important Dates	Events
Notes	Follow-up
Provider Evaluation/Rating	

Figure 4.1 • Partnership Development form

DIGITAL PARTNERSHIPS FOR CAREER AWARENESS—LONG-TERM PLANNING						
Name of Partner or Content Provider	Curriculum/ Topic	Career Objective	Organization	Contact	Email	Notes

Figure 4.2 • Digital Partnerships form

Chapter 5

Extending Career Options for Rural Students

IN 2005, the Southern Oregon Education Service District (SOESD) was awarded a USDA Rural Utility Services grant. The vision of technology supervisor Jay Matheson, his insights, and his grant-writing skills resulted in a three-year distance learning program: Extending Career Options for Rural Students (ECORS).

The ESD is located in Medford, Oregon, and serves 13 school districts, 100 buildings in three counties across approximately 10,000 square miles in the southwestern part of the state. The service area includes 3,500 teachers and 50,000 students. Matheson developed the project in response to a lack of resources in these rural school districts.

People in the community were expressing their frustration with the high dropout rates. At the same time, there was a documented low-interest level in technology programs in most of the small, high-poverty schools. On the national level, reports indicated an increased demand and high-income potential in technology-related fields, but it was clear that access to these careers was going to be difficult for local students living and learning in remote school districts with limited funds.

In the context of this project, extending career options meant simply using videoconferencing and other digital communication technologies to broaden students' understanding of what kinds of careers existed in the STEM fields. The idea of using videoconferencing and web-based instruction to provide rural K–12 students with cultural opportunities and exposure to a variety of career paths was seen by Jay and other project collaborators as a way students could discover more possibilities for their own lives. They would be given a chance to get an up-close look at real jobs in science, math, engineering, and technology fields. Most importantly, they could develop relationships with professionals already working in these career fields.

"In these rural mountain towns, students aren't often exposed to adult role models beyond their teachers, doctors, grocery store clerks, bank clerks, or gas station attendants," says Matheson. Several of the participating schools are located hours away from the nearest urban area, and though their local communities are rich in many ways, opportunities for schoolchildren are limited and dropout rates are alarmingly high. And, as in most schools, budgets are being slashed and field trips to science centers and museums are all but history. In addition, because of the long distances, a visit from a working scientist or a technology mentor is out of the question. Through the ECORS project, these students could begin to imagine a future outside the realm of their own day-to-day experiences.

The federal grant monies made it possible to purchase videoconference equipment and hire a professional technology integration trainer. Participating teachers in 17 schools and as many as 5,000 students benefited in numerous ways including training in the use of interactive videoconferencing (IVC), digital media (Web 2.0) technologies, and training and support for adapting new instructional strategies, including career extension projects. Before this project, most of the schools had had no access to the technology or to the training.

As a bonus, the number of sites receiving new equipment (mobile interactive videoconference units) was nearly doubled by a state-funded technology grant.

Two of the participating districts then undertook major network improvement projects, bringing high-speed fiberoptic-based broadband to schools that had been using only a single T1 line, increasing the scope and the reach of the project.

To support participating teachers, project leaders developed an online community using both the IVC equipment and existing Internet infrastructure and equipment. More than 300 teachers received technical support and training in the operation and use of IVC and Web 2.0 tools through a WebCT online instruction project and through face-to-face training—two annual summer "CyberFairs" and a weekly Virtual Office Hours meeting via videoconferencing. Over time, a virtual professional community of learning developed. The combined training modalities also served as a model for blended learning strategies.

The Grant

In the fall of 2005, the SOESD was awarded a USDA Rural Utilities Services grant to fund the three-year career extension project. Schools in all three ESD service counties received videoconferencing equipment to provide, and eventually expand, career awareness for 5,000 students. The grant also provided resources to train as many as 300 teachers in the operation, integration, and application of interactive videoconferencing in the classroom.

Project Goals

The long-term goal of the ECORS project was to introduce rural K–12 students living in remote, low-income areas to a broad range of cultural opportunities and to provide exposure to a variety of career paths, particularly in the STEM fields.

Participating teachers used the WebCT training platform to access the project facilitator (this author) and each other. They also used WebCT to access and work their way through a step-by-step online guide in the use of videoconferencing and Web 2.0 tools. As part of the work, they also learned ways they could use digital media tools—blogs and wikis—to connect their students with extended career development activities. Teachers earned "eBuck$" rewards (see Figure 5.1) upon demonstrating a level of proficiency and involvement with the technologies. They used their eBuck$ to purchase virtual field trips from the Center for Interactive Learning and Collaboration (CILC; www.cilc.org).

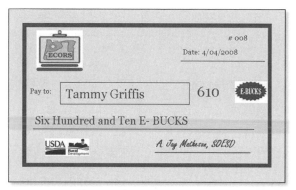

Figure 5.1 eBuck$ proves that even modest rewards can be motivating

Proficiency included making real videoconference connections, developing appropriate lesson plans, participating in the online environment, creating personal blogs, contributing to the project wiki, and generating virtual partnerships with content providers and STEM professionals. Once teachers were ready, students took virtual field trips to places they once would have only looked at in books or on a website. Because videoconferencing is live, they could interact with scientists and ask questions about their work and their careers. Some were able to augment what they were learning in the classroom with videoconference workshops run by experts in that field.

About CILC

The Center for Interactive Learning and Collaboration is an online databank of more than 200 videoconference content providers including museums, education service centers, digital learning networks, science centers, universities, and individual professional providers and educators. In addition to an extensive directory of virtual field trips, CILC offers professional development in the use of videoconferencing, academic classes and workshops, and a place where teachers can arrange classroom-to-classroom collaborations—all through the application of videoconferencing.

Building a Community of Learning

The project's professional learning community was first established during a daylong face-to-face meeting, or CyberFair, that took place in the summertime before the start of the school year. The two-year project would require teachers in all corners of this mountainous, far-flung area to communicate and collaborate on a regular basis throughout the school year and the one to follow. Once the online community was established, participants would help each other learn to use the equipment and solve problems. They relied on the remote facilitator (this author), who was located in another part of the state, for daily support. Those who attended the first face-to-face meeting would help others in their local schools learn about the opportunities that the new videoconference technology offered—how to use the equipment and participate in the project—a train-the-trainer model. For every new member the early adopters brought aboard over the school year, they earned eBuck$ for virtual field trips. Motivators were built into the program from the start.

CyberFair

Teachers who attended the CyberFair were typically pioneer types, or early adopters, and represented all the schools that would participate. Each made a commitment to share the project, the resources, and the innovation with other teachers in their schools. To establish the framework of their widespread community of learning, they spent part of the day establishing expectations and ground rules. Together, they answered questions about how they would act as change agents in their local schools. They agreed that effective leadership strategies included:

- Modeling new behaviors
- Mentoring others in innovation
- Accessing and sharing resources
- Reaching out to the greater community to keep them informed
- Developing partnerships
- Collaborating consistently with project leaders

The daylong meeting consisted of a large-group session where potential technology facilitators and leaders were introduced to the project and, together, set baseline standards for their group; a virtual meeting with the state's regional science center, OMSI; and breakout sessions covering the project, videoconferencing, digital media applications, and technology leadership skills.

After lunch, breakout sessions provided instruction in the videoconference technology, virtual field trips, digital media applications, and more dialogue about what leadership means in the context of technology adoption in schools and districts. The leadership sessions were based on ISTE's Technology Leadership Standards (www.iste.org/Libraries/PDFs/2001_Technology_Leadership_Standards_Doc.sflb.ashx).

The Equipment

The ESD designed and implemented, for each participating school, a set of two custom mobile IVC solutions, one of which included an IVC codec camera, microphones, VCR/DVD player, document camera, and a video projector. One unit, based on the Tandberg 770 MXP codec, provided a mobile multimedia teaching/learning station that moved from classroom to classroom. A smaller Polycom VSX 3000 allowed administrators and teachers to conduct district and regional meetings without having to leave the building.

Digital Tools

Videoconferencing, the WebCT online learning platform, and the Web 2.0 applications supported collaboration among teacher participants. Synchronous and asynchronous forums were established for guest speakers, content experts, mentors, class-to-class partnerships, and business and industry partnerships. Teachers made use of the blogs to reflect about their participation in the project and share with other participants what they were doing in their own classrooms with digital media and distance learning applications. The project wiki provided a forum where teachers could share best practices as the project progressed. Several teachers picked up on the Web 2.0 applications right away. One fifth grade language arts teacher designed a class wiki to support a classroom literary project. Others used the wiki and blog tools to support instructional goals in addition to the career awareness activities. Without the ECORS project activities—providing a context for using these tools—these teachers most likely would not have been introduced to the Web 2.0 technologies. Many had to find ways to work around firewalls and application blocks. All were determined to proceed once they discovered the power of these digital tools—once they got a taste of their students' enthusiasm and appreciation. Some of the teachers went in kicking and screaming, but they all were becoming members of the new digital community.

From then on, project participants communicated through the web-based and videoconferencing programs setup and supported by project leaders at the ESD (and the remote project facilitator). The online WebCT learning platform site—or ECORS Project Guide—provided discussion boards, an online Community Clubhouse site (a kind of project homeroom), a project calendar, and email, fostering regular communication. Teachers created blogs to self-reflect and share experiences. Links to the teacher blogs were posted on the WebCT site. A model wiki was employed to give teachers a forum where they could share best practices and where they could practice using this new tool. At first, many of the teachers were reluctant to use the digital media. Though they had heard of blogs, most were certain blogging was not for them. But once a few discovered how easy it was, and then posted links to their blogs on the online community site, others followed. They were learning skills that many of their students used at home every day. They were beginning to speak the language of their students.

Students need personally meaningful, hands-on experiences in order to become fully engaged. Learning environments need to be relevant to be meaningful. The same could be said for teachers learning to use Web 2.0 tools in the context of this project. They were applying the tools in meaningful ways instead of being told to do so for the sake of learning how to videoconference, blog, or create a classroom wiki.

Although professional development communities of learning are traditionally more commonplace in a face-to-face environment, this project proved to its participants that virtual communities are also possible. Participants learned the power of digital connectivity.

The first field trips were meant to gain practice and were not limited to STEM providers and themes. ECORS students enjoyed live, face-to-face workshops with professionals and programs all over the country, including:

- COSI (Center of Science and Industry in Columbus, Ohio)
- Columbia Gorge Museum
- Oregon Museum of Science and Industry (OMSI)
- Expedition Northwest
- Baseball Hall of Fame
- Cleveland Museum of Art
- Carnegie Museum of Natural History
- Cape May County Park & Zoo
- Challenger Learning Center
- Smithsonian Art Museum
- NASA
- Alaska Sea Life Center

Baseline surveys on interest in and use of videoconferencing technology were applied at the initial face-to-face meeting and again at project's end. Results of the surveys are provided later in this chapter.

Teacher Training

The online instructional modules supported the ECORS Learning Community, over the life of the project, through two self-guided instructional modules. Guide One offered teachers instructional strategies for the implementation of interactive videoconferencing and Web 2.0 tools in the classroom. Teachers learned about the history of videoconferencing, how to set up and use the equipment, and best practices for designing instruction: lesson plans, presentation, room configuration, and student evaluation.

Guide Two provided instruction in ways they could use these technology tools and digital applications to extend career awareness for their students.

The Project

The project took off at the beginning of the 2006–07 school year. Participating schools were provided with mobile IVC units that could be moved from classroom to classroom and customized for optimal use.

ECORS Learning Community teachers practiced videoconferencing with each other, honing strategies and practices to integrate IVC into their classroom learning plans. As the project progressed, a weekly Virtual Office Hours via IVC brought ECORS teachers and administrators together. Virtual Office Hours were facilitated by project leaders at the ESD. This provided a platform to share and problem-solve and practice using the equipment.

Once they became comfortable with the technology, teachers planned virtual field trips to science, research, and technology centers through CILC. The CILC website and content provider database made it easier for teachers to find content providers and classroom presenters because they were all organized in one place on the CILC site. Teachers could search by topic or by workshop name. CILC also provided training and support in use of videoconferencing in the classroom.

The weekly live, face-to-face interactive videoconference sessions, or Virtual Office Hours, provided teachers and administrators a chance to talk informally about issues, ideas, and questions about the technology and the project in general. It also gave them a chance to practice using videoconferencing. Sometimes just hearing what others were doing or learning how someone else solved a technical issue was all that teachers needed to get unstuck.

One of the prevalent issues was time. With the pressure to meet NCLB standards and requirements, project teachers had little extra time for innovation and the training, practice, and planning that went with trying something new, even though the project had the potential to enhance critical instructional goals. As the project progressed, the time issue became a bigger factor. Also, there was little, if any, support from local or state administrators to add career education to the curriculum, even though everyone seemed to think it was a great idea. Project leaders found themselves competing with reading and math marching orders, "and that's really no competition when your scores on reading and math are in the newspaper," lamented one ECORS administrator.

Another recurring issue for the rural schools was reliability of the network connectivity. It was not unusual in some of the districts for a classroom to be all set for a virtual field trip, only to discover that the network was down or overloaded with data, Internet usage, or other videoconferences. One or two failed videoconferences could leave teachers and their students disappointed, discouraged, and not likely to try one more time.

But to the credit of these teachers, they persisted, and the online professional learning community and the weekly live discussion groups provided a problem-solving forum and opportunity to develop a level of comfort and expertise in both the setup and use of videoconferencing and the pursuit of the goals of the project.

As the project evolved, the secondary project goal of familiarizing and training teachers in use of digital media became less of a burden for the teachers. After earning eBuck$ for creating blogs or wiki notations or for adding to the online discussion, they soon felt like professional bloggers, and many expressed pride in their accomplishments as role models in the digital age. They had become empowered in their use of digital media as part of their classroom instruction.

In addition to the pre-project two-day summertime training meeting, project leaders visited each school in the fall, before the start of the project, to provide training in the setup and use of the videoconference equipment. Those who received the training followed the train-the-trainer turnkey model.

Guide One

After completing a virtual tutorial on how to use WebCT, teachers learned through an online class about the history of distance learning, gaining a perspective on videoconferencing, online learning, and Web 2.0 that set the stage and provided the context in which they would be gaining skills and enhancing classroom instruction. They were introduced to the benefits of using videoconferencing and digital media tools in the classroom.

The class was designed so that teachers could work their way through progressive modules at their own pace, earning eBuck$ rewards as they went, redeemable for virtual field trips. Their enthusiasm over the eBuck$ rewards reinforced the project leadership's belief in the power of motivators for teacher training in technology adoption.

Examples of tasks that could earn eBuck$ included working with tech-support staff to set up the mobile videoconference cart and host a practice session, conducting a second practice session that included video projector and document camera feedback on the project blog, and participating in a videoconference planning session.

Once introduced to the project, teachers were provided with step-by-step instructions—learning at their own pace—in setting up videoconferencing equipment, scheduling IVC sessions, troubleshooting connectivity and equipment issues, preparing instructional strategies, and developing ideas for innovation using the tools. Copy-me templates were posted for download, including student evaluation forms, equipment setup checklists, lesson plans, videoconference scripts, instructional planning, and network scheduling checklists.

In addition to the project and technology tutorials, participants were given instruction, guidelines, and downloadable templates to support local community outreach and public relations. They had access to templates and step-by-step guidance in writing press releases and newsletter articles, speaking to community groups, and establishing community partnerships. The purpose here was to help schools keep parents and communities informed with an eye to keeping the project going, once the grant money was exhausted, through community support at the local level.

Teachers learned from each other by reading each other's blogs and discussion board entries. As is often common in these kinds of groups, there were a few who took the lead and were the most vocal. In terms of facilitating a virtual learning community, this author learned the importance of acknowledging the front-runners, but also the need to bring out the lurkers and try to lure them into the groups. Teachers also made use of the project wiki to share lessons learned over time. The online site served as a teachers' lounge and project bulletin board, as well as a place where everyone could learn and participate at their own pace.

Online content also included a calendar, resource links, and vignettes contributed by other teachers around the country. In addition to the online content, a video stream of the weekly Virtual Office Hours sessions was posted each week on the community page so that no one ever had to miss anything because of time constraints. Many would probably agree that after a long school day, the last thing they want to do is watch an hour-long video about videoconference issues. Nevertheless, the material was always there and always available.

Guide Two

The second guide, in addition to the discussion boards, community page, resource links, calendar of events, project templates, teacher blog links, and project wiki, provided:

- Oregon-based science/math/technology content integrated into training curriculum

- Nontraditional career options and opportunities for female (and male) students

- An application portion for both elementary and secondary students:
  - Elementary students used IVC as a virtual career education textbook, connecting with experts and role models;
  - Middle school students used IVC for career exploration options with a variety of organizations and institutions not available to them locally;
  - High school students used IVC to focus on specific careers and to connect with mentors and role models within those career pathways.

Teachers were able to work their way in steps through the project by completing each step of the guides and then cashing in earned eBuck$ for virtual field trips. They learned how to guide students through virtual field trips and to apply use of the technology to other parts of the curriculum.

Results

As a result of the online training and its 24/7 availability for those who could participate from home, teachers had access at all times to a professional learning community. They could take their time to prepare and plan. They used their blogs to collaborate with each other. They took advantage of the online facilitator to ask questions when they felt stuck. The results of the project were astounding for many who may have felt a sense of reluctance at the beginning when they realized they would have to work outside their comfort zone. Following are some of the project results as reported by project leaders.

- Teachers increased their comfort level and gained proficiency in the use of the IVC equipment and the application of Web 2.0 tools for planning and instruction.

- Numerous successful IVC connections, sessions, and events were conducted over the life of the project and beyond. (Many of the teachers who had never used IVC before, and who had been reluctant adopters, were eager to continue using IVC as part of their instructional strategies.)

- Participants honed their IVC presentation techniques, content sharing ideas, and communication skills with the help of remote-site collaborators, expanding the boundaries of their classrooms and their learning community.

- Students were provided with opportunities to participate in and learn about the appropriate use of IVC technologies.

- Teachers learned techniques for managing IVC activities including discussions, collaborations, and instruction. They learned by reviewing best practices on the online learning platform, followed by real-time application; by meeting virtually with their peers to discuss issues, solutions, and ideas; and by discovering firsthand how the tools enhanced their curriculum.

- Assistance was provided for creating lesson plans using IVC to extend career awareness and exploration activities. Teachers won free virtual field trips for following through with the lesson plans and creating excitement and engagement among their students.

- Training was ongoing and accessible 24/7, supporting teachers whenever they had time to participate.

- Statewide partnerships and collaborations were formed with regional science centers such as OMSI, Oregon Health and Science University (OHSU), Intel, and the Columbia Gorge Museum, resulting in focused science, math, and technology career content experiences for students as well as professional development for teachers.

Pre- and post-surveys of participating teachers showed a 50% gain in technical knowledge and skills related to completing the ECORS project activities. Participating teachers were requested to ask themselves questions such as these as they progressed through the ECORS Project:

- What are your goals for the project in terms of student outcomes?

- To what extent will use of the technology be part of the lessons?

- How will you connect the content of the ECORS project with existing curriculum?

- How do you believe this project will benefit your students?

Through pre- and post-surveys and other project evaluation tools, project leaders reported that as many as 90% of student participants showed significant change or improvement in the following ways:

- Through the integration of the videoconferencing and digital media technologies, students increased and enriched their options for career awareness, career exploration, and career-related learning experiences.

- Female students expanded their options and awareness in fields of math, science, engineering, and technology in ways they might not have without the access to role models they gained through the program.

- Teachers were able to help their students acquire new knowledge, skills, and attitudes in ways they might not otherwise have been able to do and in ways that would help these students reach their full career potential.

- Local communities in this extremely rural area were beginning to notice fewer dropouts and more students enrolling in professional technical education fields as they went on to college; more female students were pursuing instruction in STEM curriculum and pursuing those fields of study beyond high school.

- The participating teachers learned how to use digital tools and how to apply distance learning technologies.

Students had access to leading-edge career-related content and professionals:

- Each participating classroom had access to cultural opportunities and exposure to a variety of career path experiences.

- Students met virtually with a wide range of people, places, and content otherwise not accessible to them in their remote, rural classrooms.

- They met with experts in math, science, and technology and discovered career options they may never before have imagined.

- Students expanded their career potential through exposure to a variety of real-world career paths; this benefited everyone, but especially female students who might never have considered these career pathways for themselves (www.engineergirl.org).

- Students linked up with role models and career mentors.

INTERVIEW

Jay Matheson

Jay Matheson is the coordinator of technology and media services at Southern Oregon Education Service District. Technology and Media Services provides a communications hub for these Oregon schools. The SOESD provides Internet access, an IVC network, and a cable television station that covers Klamath, Josephine, and Jackson counties.

Prior to his work in Oregon implementing innovative distance-learning programs regionally and statewide, Jay helped launch a flagship distance-learning program with CILC. There, he was the first distance-learning coordinator in Indiana and went on to become the national director of outreach for CILC.

Jay's project, ECORS, and my role as facilitator were the inspiration for this book. Jay had a sense early on, before STEM issues came to the fore in education conversations, that exposing rural students to career models was a critical initiative for 21st-century learning. During his work in the late 1990s helping get CILC off the ground, he also came to understand the power of face-to-face videoconferencing in building relationships between students and mentors or role models. It was, in his mind, the perfect tool for building career awareness and classroom partnerships.

Camille: How did you first come upon the idea for the ECORS project?

Jay: Oftentimes, necessity is the mother of invention. We needed new video-conferencing equipment and I saw this project as a way to replace the old ones. I've also always had a soft spot for career education, and especially for kids in rural areas who don't have the same exposure that kids have in more suburban or urban areas. So out of those two needs came ECORS.

I've worked in a variety of settings in three different states. There are a lot of differences between urban and rural kids, but there are also a lot of similarities—and one of those is the lack of the interaction that kids need in order to expand their possibilities.

Camille: Since its completion, have any of the participating schools continued using the technology?

Jay: There's actually been a spread of the use of the technology—beyond the rural end users. Teachers were talking about their experience in the ECORS project, and then teachers in the less rural areas wanted those experiences for their kids. So the administrators wanted to upgrade for equal opportunity.

Camille: What are some of the simple ways—without adding a lot of prep time for teachers—that kids can access career awareness in the STEM fields as part of core-content studies?

Jay: We tried to build that into career extensions by using kids' natural curiosity about people—I don't know if kids are really very curious about jobs, but they are curious about adults and what adults do, so we're trying to play on that. The content might have been science or math related, but then to spend some time allowing kids to do that natural kind of chatter with the presenter.

The teacher could even say, Let's brainstorm three questions to get this started: How did you get to be a marine biologist? How much money do you make? Where did you go to school for that?

There's a natural curiosity that young people have—because in their minds they're going to be doing some of those things. You never know when you're going to come across an interest in a child. Let's try and give kids as many options as we can about when that interest might get challenged—and relationships start to develop.

One of the cool things about videoconferencing is that once I've sat and chatted with you for an hour in a videoconference, I have a relationship with you, a relationship with the narrator (presenter) of the videoconference. There's a comfort level—there were some middle school students talking with a young woman who works at Eli Lilly. She started telling them—the content was about health—but the kids were really interested in her. They started asking her questions, very personal questions, and at that point she had become comfortable enough to say some things to them and she talked about how she started being interested in this in middle school—she made sure her grades were good enough and in high school she took some courses she needed and then went on to college. So it's not coming from their parents, or teachers, it's coming from someone in the real world so it carries more weight.

Camille: So in a way, the inspiration may not have as much to do with the subject matter as it has to do with the person they look up to.

Jay: Exactly right. The stuff they're getting is not just career content but career process. They may come from families that don't have the experience of going off to college—their families continue to live not far from where they were born.

We focused in part on minorities and women. It's only been maybe in the last 30 years that as a society we've begun to recognize the problems that minorities and women have in the workplace. In most of our history as humankind, women have not had the same opportunities as men, and even now it's one step forward and one step back.

Camille: Knowing what you know now, are there ways you would alter the career awareness elements of the project?

Jay: I think it went the way we wanted it to. I did make some assumptions about what teachers were aware of—we should have maybe been more explicit about the career process. They could have been more intentional about building the relationships.

Camille: Because teachers are somewhat isolated in the classroom, what are some of the ways they can stay current in STEM career trends?

Jay: That's one of the places where we are missing the boat in terms of getting information to teachers. The amount of information has just exploded, and teachers need to be up on those career trends, but how do you do that when some of those careers didn't even exist last year? The same curiosity we're trying to instill in the kids, teachers need to model. So the question becomes: How do you help a person whose career track is essentially nonexistent? There really isn't a career track for teachers—research doesn't show that after three years of teaching there's any difference in student outcomes. If you accept that the difference between a teacher who has taught for three or four years and a brand new teacher is null, then you have to say what's wrong with this system? Why is it that in a system where we believe in lifelong learning, teachers don't get better and better? I think that's because we don't challenge them after that point, we allow people to move into a career track where they raise their salary essentially by staying in the job.

Camille: Maybe there's a certain amount of discouragement.

Jay: Oh, a tremendous amount. We have not built in incentives to encourage the curiosity and those incentives—How many administrators can you have in a building? How many reading specialists? What I'm saying is, if people were more interested in their own careers, I think they would be more attuned to where other careers are going. Where we're missing the boat is after the first five years, teachers should have a sabbatical. You go out and work in a different setting—go see what kind of learning kids are really going to need when they leave school. If you want teachers to continue to grow, let them have a chance to develop their curiosity. You can only do that by getting out of the classroom setting. In the setting, the job is so demanding—there's so little time to do growth and teach at the same time. We don't expect people in the military, when we send them out to battle, to be honing their military skills. You come back for R&R. You don't do R&R in the middle of your mission.

Let private enterprise be the teachers for a while for some of these folks and give them a chance to reflect—come back to the classroom with a new curiosity. Let them connect to the world via videoconferencing with their classroom and teach their kids what they learned right from the workplace.

Are you familiar with the Big Dig? The project that went on underneath Boston? About 15 years ago, to deal with the traffic mess in Boston, they decided to dig tunnels underneath the city. There were a couple of schools that built their curriculum around the Big Dig. Those kids studied the Big Dig for years. All their science, and all their math, and all their reading all connected to what was going on in the Big Dig. So why couldn't you do that on a smaller scale? Teacher by teacher, if we made these connections with the teachers and the outside world— create lessons that connects teaching with a particular place or event. It could be a national park, it could be a nonprofit effort to feed Haitians—it doesn't have to be a business.

Camille: And the technology supports that work.... Do you believe videoconferencing, like some say, is on its way out in favor of commercial online apps?

Jay: If you're there to build relationships, videoconferencing is a community tool, as opposed to a personal tool. It's perfect for the large group experience, the classroom experience.

Camille: With the cost of higher ed rising and so many students unable to afford to go to college, how are we going to accommodate those kids?

Jay: I'm not sure higher ed is really very good at helping people with most careers. I remember when I was going to school, the engineering students were overburdened—another five hours of classes plus with extra courses—and when they got out and went to work, say, at Dow Chemical, they'd send them back to school for two years to learn the stuff they wanted them to know. My sense is that colleges aren't really the place to do a lot of career stuff.

We need some alternatives. We see some of the private sector stepping in, say, in the technical field. Technical schools like ITT. That's a model. There are many people doing entry-level jobs that don't see the potential of a career ladder. Those kind of trade schools—they are less expensive, more focused. They're for students who got out of high school and lived a little bit and are serious about their education—we could broaden what they do. Even students that attend some college could benefit from schools along this model. I'm just not sure that higher ed changes course fast enough to be is the best place to develop careers. I'm thinking of how students could learn invention and design—in academic settings when creative thinking is not encouraged, it's discouraged. We will have a hard time competing with the applied science power of China and India. They have so many more gifted students than we have total students.

So we need to look more broadly in our emphasis on STEM. My sense is that if we only encourage students to view STEM narrowly, we will have missed something in terms of the value of the American experiment—the melting pot aspect of who we are. Part of the reason American style appeals to the world is that we are already a world market. The U.S. is a mix of so many cultures. Our educational process needs to find ways to build off the energy that comes from the blending of cultures. We need to use that energy to fuel the invention and design of products for the whole world. We have this window of opportunity to help structure the future of the world market. It isn't just going to happen. Look at the Danes, who are now known for amazing furniture design—they have worked hard to gain that type of world recognition. We will need to do the same.

Camille: So you're saying use the world as a classroom.

Jay: Yes. That's what videoconferencing allows us to do—we can connect students to the employer across town or in another state. I think we haven't really begun to explore what that could mean to us. What if we placed teachers in other countries for a period of time and one of the things they do is develop a series of videoconferences to share what they are learning with students and other teachers? Using IVC like that could enhance teaching skills and build world-class content at the same time.

Chapter 6

Funding Ideas

Not everything that can be counted counts,
and not everything that counts
can be counted.

—Albert Einstein

THIS IS NOT A BOOK on fund-raising or grant writing, but I, your humble author, am an occasional education grant writer, a former development officer, and a longtime resource networker who almost 20 years ago launched a column titled "Grants and Contests and Other Good Deals" in *Technology & Learning* magazine. I understand that funding is one of the biggest challenges for school reform. What could be more important as we prepare young people to prosper in a digitally connected global world, as we strive to fulfill our hopes and dreams, than finding the resources to pull it off?

I recommend that as you begin exposing your students to STEM careers and professionals, and to career awareness more generally, you start on a small, manageable scale. As we'll explore in Chapter 7, there are many, many free and low-cost Web 2.0 technologies that you can begin using immediately to expose your students to STEM information and role models.

Eventually, though, you may start to think bigger ... and that's great! It also means that you might need to start looking for funding.

Types of projects commonly eligible for educational funding include curriculum development, technology integration, teacher training, student projects, and technology acquisition. Funders almost always favor projects and programs that are innovative and sustainable, that leverage existing resources, and that demonstrate efforts to leverage funds through partnerships. STEM-related projects and programs are currently extremely hot—do not hesitate to highlight this angle when applying for grants.

In the old days, one had to spend days at the public library combing through foundation directories at the Foundation Center collection for grants guidelines and funding criteria. Today, there are tens of thousands of private and corporate funds, endowments, foundations, and myriad giving programs whose areas of interest include education. There are contests for students and teachers. There are awards programs. Some of them are national, some regional, some for school districts and classrooms. Today, it's almost all available online. Still, hunting for funding opportunities, even online, is a lot of work.

IF YOU DON'T ASK,
the answer is "no."

There are numerous online education newsletters providing information about funding sources, such as the *Pen Weekly Newsblast*, *eSchoolNews*, and *Teacher Magazine*. There are also numerous blogs and websites offering guidance, information, and resources for funding education projects.

Specialty search engines may also help you in your search for the right funders for your STEM and/or technology-integration project. You can begin collecting bookmarked links to search engines and mega-lists specific to your funding purpose. For example, use keywords from your own project to search the SearchEdu website (www.searchedu.com) for press releases and project descriptions.

On the following pages you'll find lists that demonstrate examples of potential funding sources: corporate and government donations, private foundation grants, corporate foundations, and other special funding programs for schools and classrooms. By no means is this an exhaustive list; rather, it is the tip of a giant iceberg of educational funding opportunities. If you are creative and persevere, there are opportunities to fund large, multiyear, district-wide projects and programs—and there are also opportunities for small classroom- or building-level projects or programs. The key to success is knowing where to look and how to make your program stand out above all the rest.

Fund-raising is a process that builds on the work you and your partners commit to over time. There are successes and failures, but every attempt is worth the time. One failure gains hard-earned lessons that inform future funding searches. As my grandfather used to say: "If you don't ask, the answer is no."

Product Donations (and Other Free Stuff)

These sources are undoubtedly general and not explicitly STEM related. However, you may need to build your infrastructure before you can make use of the more specific grants and funding opportunities.

Computers for Learning
http://computersforlearning.gov

> This program donates surplus federal computer equipment to schools and educational nonprofit organizations, especially to those in need. Any public, private, or homeschool K–12 school is eligible for the preowned equipment.

Federal Resources for Educational Excellence
www.free.ed.gov

> At this site you can find free materials from government agencies including animations, documents, videos, photos, and other resources organized by curriculum. Dozens of agencies participate in this bank of federally supported teaching and learning resources for almost every curriculum category. They have a lessons-learned section contributed to by educators who have already participated. Sign up for an RSS feed or find them on Twitter.

FETC Virtual Conference and Expo
http://fetc.org/events/virtual-conference/home.aspx

> The FETC Virtual Conference and Expo is now available free on demand. Find here the latest developments in 21st-century skills professional development best practices.

Gifts in Kind International
www.giftsinkind.org

> Thousands of companies contribute in-kind gifts and products to a network of 50,000 charities, and these contributions are available to organizations such as schools that register and pay an annual fee of $125–250.

Slideshare
www.slideshare.net

> Slideshare's website offers free, downloadable interactive lessons, usable with whiteboard.

Special Programs for Classrooms and Teachers

AIAA: Science and Math Program Grants
www.aiaa.org/content.cfm?pageid=216

> The American Institute of Aeronautics and Astronautics offers classroom grants for science and math programs to assist educators who present mathematics, science, and technology principles to K–12 students in demonstrated engaging and hands-on ways in order to inspire and motivate future aeronautics and aerospace engineers, scientists, pilots, and space explorers.

Amgen/NSTA: New Science Teacher Academy
www.nsta.org/academy/

> A professional development initiative for high school or middle school science teachers, the academy was created to help encourage quality science teaching, to assist in developing teacher confidence through these experiences, and to perfect teacher content knowledge.

Big Deal Books
www.bigdealbook.com

If you subscribe to their online newsletter, you will be in the know, and this group will have done all the work for you! How great is that? Though their focus is on ELL and technology, their resources are rich with sources of grants, funding opportunities, other free newsletters, STEM information and sources, and a host of 21st-century themes, including current events such as the recent Gulf oil spill and ways students can learn about going green. Look for the Big Deal Book of Technology.

Engineering Design Challenges
http://edc.nasa.gov

Sponsored by NASA, this program challenges students to understand problems faced by NASA engineers and design solutions in the area of aerospace systems. Students work with teachers and parents.

Gloria Barron Prize for Young Heroes
www.barronprize.org

Students ages 8–18 can win up to $2,500 as recognized leaders who have contributed to their communities by protecting the health and sustainability of the environment.

Honeywell: Educators at Space Academy (Middle School)
www.spacecamp.com/educators/honeywell/
http://honeywell.com/Citizenship/Pages/science-math-education.aspx

Honeywell prides itself as being a supporter of STEM education and proliferation in K–12 schools. They prove their commitment through programs such as the Space Academy for middle school science and math teachers. This program funds scholarships for these teachers, covering five days at the U.S. Space and Rocket Center in Huntsville, Alabama. Recipients get 40 hours of intensive classroom, laboratory, and training time, where they focus on space science and space exploration. They also participate in astronaut-style training, simulations, and activities meant to promote life-long learning.

MIT: Lemelson-MIT InvenTeams

http://web.mit.edu/inventeams/about.html

An innovative professional development program for high school science, math, and technology teachers and their students, its goal is to foster inventiveness. Project teams collaborate to identify a problem, research the problem, and then develop a prototype invention as an in-class or extra-curricular project in order to solve the problem.

National Audubon Society: Pennies for the Planet

www.togethergreen.org/p4p/Educators.aspx

Students can get involved with conservation by taking part in local conservation action projects, and by collecting and sending in pennies for national and worldwide conservation projects. National Audubon Society staff visit prize-winning schools to help create a program about wildlife and wild places.

National Council of Teachers of Mathematics (NCTM): Mathematics Education Trust Grants and Awards

www.nctm.org/resources/content.aspx?id=198

The mission of NCTM's Mathematics Education Trust is to "channel the generosity of contributors through the creation and funding of grants, awards, honors, and other projects that support the improvement of mathematics teaching and learning." At this site you can find grants, scholarships, and awards grouped by grade.

NCTM: Engaging Students in Learning Mathematics Grant for Grades 6–8 Teachers

www.nctm.org/resources/content.aspx?id=1320

Grants of up to $3,000 are provided to classroom teachers who are members, or whose schools are members, and who currently make creative use of materials to engage students in learning experiences that will deepen and enhance mathematics content knowledge.

NCTM: Using Music to Teach Math Grants for Grades PK–2 Teachers

www.nctm.org/resources/content.aspx?id=1318

National Council of Teachers of Mathematics make these grants of up to $3,000 for member teachers who incorporate music into the elementary school classroom to help young students learn mathematics.

NEA Foundation: Student Achievement Grants
www.neafoundation.org/programs/StudentAchievement_Guidelines.htm

> The NEA Foundation funds teachers and other education professionals up to
> $5,000 for those who promote student achievement by helping them engage
> in critical thinking and problem solving to deepen their knowledge of any
> standards-based subject matter.

NSTA/Ciba Specialty Chemicals—
Exemplary Middle and High School Science Teaching Awards
www.nsta.org/pdfs/557.pdf

> Full-time classroom teachers are eligible for these awards of up to $1,000
> that recognize teachers who have demonstrated exemplary science teaching
> in: creativity using science teaching materials; design and use of innova-
> tive teaching plans and ideas; and development and implementation of
> department, school, or school-community programs that improve science
> instruction and/or stimulate interest in science and the learning of science.
> Maximum award: $4,000, a one-year membership in the National Science
> Teachers Association (NSTA), and up to $1,000 to attend the NSTA National
> Conference on Science Education.

NSTA: Distinguished Service to Science Education Award
www.nsta.org/pdfs/awards/DistinguishedService.pdf

> This award recognizes extraordinary contributions to science education
> by paying up to $500 of the recipient's travel costs to the NSTA National
> Conference.

Government Grants
and Funding Programs

One of the first places to look for opportunities, application forms, and guidance for government grants is Grants.gov (www.grants.gov), which is run by the
Department of Health and Human Services. Here you will find a complete listing
of all government grants, guidelines, and applications for all the federal agencies.

Another go-to site, updated daily, is the Federal Register (www.gpoaccess.
gov/fr). Published by the Federal Register, the National Archives, and Records

Administration, the site provides a complete listing of regulations connected to all federal programs.

E-Rate
www.usac.org/sl
www.usac.org/sl/about/overview-program.aspx

A commonly used name for the Schools and Libraries Program of the Universal Service Fund, E-Rate is a telecommunications funding program providing schools and libraries with discounts on Internet connectivity and some related purposes. Schools must apply each year and must have a district technology plan. The process is burdensome and usually handled by district IT departments. Because the funds relieve some of the burden of having to pay for connectivity, there is, as a result, more money in school budgets to pay for equipment and training. This is a topic that has not been free of controversy, as it is increasingly complex. Dark side or not, E-Rate discounts help make it possible for many schools to participate in a connected school environment. E-Rate funding can often be used as matching funds for government grants requiring matches, or at minimum, as a way to demonstrate program sustainability.

National Science Foundation
www.nsf.gov

The NSF supports research and education in science and engineering through a variety of grants programs. They are an independent agency run by a board. Their website is rich with funding information, links to publications, and information about science-related issues in the news.

National Weather Association Sol Hirsch Education Fund Grants
www.nwas.org/grants/solhirsch.php?

This grant offers $750 for teacher enrollment in an accredited course in related study such as atmospheric sciences. The money can also be used for scientific materials or classroom materials and equipment.

Stimulus Dollars (American Recovery and Reinvestment Act)
www2.ed.gov/policy/gen/leg/recovery/programs.html

Signed into law on February 17, 2009, by President Obama, the objective of the American Recovery and Reinvestment Act was to stimulate the economy. The billions of dollars allocated for education were earmarked for programs meant to expand educational opportunities through innovative programs too lengthy to list here. The use of technology meets criteria in most of the programs to improve student achievement, staff development, and parental and community involvement. Visit this page at the Ed.gov site for a complete listing of programs and reports on spending and awards and future grant availability.

U.S. Department of Education Grants Programs
www.ed.gov/fund/landing.jhtml

This federal agency provides money to states, regional education centers, and schools to fund school reform, technology integration, and a range of federal initiatives. Some programs are available every year; some run only for one or two years at a time. This site provides links to the Federal Register, where you will find grants and contracts information and RFPs (requests for proposals). The site also offers both information for individuals seeking tuition assistance and guidelines in grants management.

USDA Rural Utility Services (RUS) Grants
www.rurdev.usda.gov/UTP_DLT.html

A federal assistance program that funds the purchase of telecommunications equipment for both education and health care programs, USDA RUS-DLT support can be used to level the playing field for rural schools, bringing required content to isolated classrooms via interactive videoconference systems and companion distance-learning equipment.

- The annual RUS-DLT equipment grant for rural and high-poverty school districts funded the Extending Career Options for Rural Students (ECORS) project featured in the case study in Chapter 5.

- Districts and regional education organizations can apply for $50,000–$500,000 in distance-learning equipment, capital expenditures toward the first-time acquisition of instructional programming, and technical assistance and instruction for using eligible equipment. Match is a required component of this grant, and highly qualified applicants that leverage local cash wisely could have substantially larger overall budgets.

Corporate and Private Foundations

Bill and Melinda Gates Foundation
www.gatesfoundation.org

> Originally endowed by Microsoft founder Bill Gates, the Bill and Melinda Gates Foundation is a family-run operation, supporting significant projects and programs around the world. In 2006, philanthropist and businessman Warren Buffett joined the organization as a trustee and doubled the initial endowments by the Gates family. In the United States, the foundation focuses on preparing students for participation and success in higher education. The foundation also supports libraries and community organizations. Gates addressed the nation's governors in 2005, calling American high schools "obsolete," adding that "training the workforce of tomorrow with the high schools of today is like trying to teach kids about today's computers on a 50-year-old mainframe." The Gates Foundation continues its efforts to make an impact on education.

Corning Incorporated Foundation
www.corning.com/about_us/corporate_citizenship/community/
corning_foundation.aspx

> Corning's foundation work includes community service programs for students, curriculum enrichment, student scholarships, facility improvement, and instructional technology projects for the classroom.

ExxonMobil
www.exxonmobil.com/Corporate/community.aspx

> Their educational focus is on math and science.

Intel Foundation: Schools of Distinction; Education Initiative
www.intel.com/education/tools

> One of several K–12 education programs sponsored by Intel, this program awards up to $25,000 to middle and high schools that have demonstrated excellence in math and science education. The Education Initiative focuses on four areas for school improvement: professional development; STEM education and professional development; supporting technology expertise at the university level; and K–12 education initiatives. In 2007, Intel and Microsoft partnered on a school-support and innovation program, Intel Teach to the Future.

John D. and Catherine T. MacArthur Foundation
www.macfound.org
www.dmlcompetition.net

The MacArthur Foundation, through its digital media and learning initiative, have feverently taken on the digital revolution for education. In December 2009, the Foundation announced a $2 million open competition for ideas to transform teaching and learning through the application of digital media in the classroom. The competition was opened to designers, educators, business-people, and researchers in hopes of creating the best learning labs of the 21st century. The goal is to help students interact, collaborate, build, and explore in new and innovative ways. Designed to promote participatory learning and STEM achievement, the competition defines participatory learning as "connecting students to individual interests and passions—inherently social in nature and occurring during hands-on, creative activities." The competition was part of MacArthur's $50 million digital media and learning initiative. The People's Choice winners were announced in June 2010. As of the writing of this book, a Game Changers Competition for kids has been announced.

Magic Johnson Foundation
www.magicjohnson.org

The Magic Johnson Foundation recently partnered with Cisco to extend distance-learning opportunities for inner-city kids and young adults. The NBA legend endowed the foundation to serve community-based organiza-tions that fund education and health projects for ethnically diverse urban populations. They help bridge the digital and social divides that can leave some kids without access to opportunities. The distance-learning programs will be part of 18 existing Empowerment Centers, funded by the foundation, around the U.S.

Michael and Susan Dell Foundation
www.msdf.org

Over a third of their grants go to support education projects. Specifically, the foundation supports strengthening administrative leadership programs for large urban schools.

Oracle Education Foundation
www.oraclefoundation.org

The Oracle Education Foundation supports three programs for K–12 education: Think.com, an online learning community for K–12 students; the 21st Century Learning Institute; and ThinkQuest, an annual competition to solve real social issues, integrating authentic curricular topics and using digital tools to create project websites. Winners participate in a live conference in San Francisco. A library of past winning projects is posted on the ThinkQuest website: www.thinkquest.org/competition/.

Raytheon's Math Moves Program
www.raytheon.com/responsibility/stem/mmu/gs/

Scholarships are provided in the amount of $1,000 to 150 middle school students nationwide to "prepare the next generation of innovators." This year, students applied scholarships to STEM summer camps or toward future college tuition. Raytheon also donates a matching grant to each winning student's school.

Siemens Foundation
www.collegeboard.com/siemens

This foundation sponsors a math and science competition that awards up to $100,000 for innovative, outstanding STEM-related projects.

Target: Field Trip Grants
https://targetfieldtripgrants.target.com/rules.php

All K–12 staff in both public and private schools are eligible for Target Field Trip Grants that provide supplemental funding up to $1,000 for all kinds of scholastic outings.

Toyota International Teacher Program
www.toyota4education.com

To support professional development in U.S. schools, Toyota International sends teachers abroad every year for two weeks to study countries that are in the forefront of dealing with environmental challenges. Teachers, administrators, and librarians are eligible to apply.

Verizon Foundation
http://foundation.verizon.com

> This foundation partners with community nonprofits to strengthen communities through health, safety, and innovative education programs. They have collaborated with Thinkfinity, for example, to fund a statewide train-the-trainer program in the state of Washington.

Grant Databases

Grant databases bring together vast amounts of information about funding sources for K–12 education programs available from private foundations, corporate foundations, and the government (local, state, and national). These databases are searchable on multiple criteria, including funding criteria, geographical restrictions, deadlines, and so on.

Edutopia Grants Information
www.edutopia.org/grant-information

> The Edutopia website, sponsored by the George Lucas Educational Foundation, hosts a well-researched list of grant information, resources, and opportunities. Their site includes links to similar sites covering listings for government grants, corporate and foundation funding opportunities, periodicals containing grant information, and technology donation programs. The listing is in blog format, garnering networking opportunities through blog posts from educators and funders.

The Foundation Center
http://foundationcenter.org

> Since 1956, the Foundation Center has helped nonprofit organizations find philanthropic dollars to support programs and special projects. Today it still maintains the most comprehensive database of U.S. grantmakers. Its publications follow trends and giving practices, and its workshops are affordable. The Foundation Center is the key location for understanding how to access grant support. Its database includes the names, addresses, contact information, areas of interest, and funding guidelines for nearly 100,000 U.S. foundations and corporate donors. The center hosts cooperating collections at many major libraries in addition to its main headquarters in New York City. The online directory is subscription based, but the ease of access makes the price

worthwhile. The foundation's publications include *Philanthropy News Digest*, *PubHub* (online collection of reports), and *Foundation Today*.

Grants for Teachers

www.grants4teachers.com

Grants for Teachers is a searchable database created for K–12 classroom teachers.

GRANTWRITING TIPS

- **Establish working partnerships.** Funders favor partnership programs where fund seekers have demonstrated they are sharing and leveraging resources and talent.

- **Build relationships with peers in cyberspace.** Web 2.0 collaboration media (social media sites) can assist you in finding potential project partners with similar project goals.

- **Keep an eye on due dates.** A really good annual funding opportunity could pass you by if you don't keep a calendar of grant proposal due dates.

- **Establish measurable goals, objectives, and outcomes.** Use these as a framework on which to build your proposal. For example, if your project involves videoconferencing with NASA scientists to improve test scores in science, how will you be able to demonstrate that the project was successful when it is completed? If you are able to articulate this in your proposal, you have just won points with the grant reader.

- **Know your audience.** Who will be reading and judging your proposal? Will it be peers in the education field or field representatives in the technology field? If it's the latter, they may not be familiar with educational jargon.

- **Keep the community informed about your successes.** Promote your classrooms and your school. A newspaper article about your school or a particular classroom is a great attachment for almost any funding proposal (unless they request that you do not include attachments).

- **Follow, to the letter, directions and guidelines for grant requests.**

Chapter 7

Tools, Tactics, Take Off! Web 2.0 Resources

Digital media are changing the way young people learn, play, and socialize.

—Henry Jenkins

Throughout this book, I've been encouraging you to use the latest digital technologies, including Web 2.0, to connect your students to STEM curriculum and professionals. The term *Web 2.0* has been defined by many people in sometimes quite different ways, to the point where many feel it has no real meaning anymore. For clarity, the definition I use here and throughout the book is quite simple: Web 2.0 technologies are interactive technologies available on the Internet. Many are free, some have their source code available (open source), and most are accessible to any school worldwide that has a sufficiently fast Internet connection.

The Tools

By now, you have probably at least heard of social media, though you may or may not be using these tools for personal and professional activities. You can be certain, however, that most students have had at least some contact with social media sites such as Facebook and YouTube.

In this chapter we will consider possible ways to use digital tools to foster and promote career awareness in STEM fields. The list of free or low-cost Web 2.0 digital applications represents the tip of an enormous interactive iceberg. These tools are readily available for teachers and students to create, communicate, and collaborate within and beyond the walls of the classroom.

Students and teachers can create materials today that in the "old days" could only be purchased from publishers or commissioned by a professional: video and audio files, books, websites, newsletters, magazines, photo albums, and electronic portfolios. Not only is the creation of professional-quality media products possible in every public school today, but the technology to support the sharing of these products with peers and professionals around the world is also at hand. Most of it is free.

There are a wealth of avenues through which to collaborate and communicate as part of the emerging digital media culture: blogs, social media sites, videoconferencing, web conferencing, instant messaging, Skype, and a variety of online community sites and tools that help to manage information, people, projects, and collaboration activities. There are too many applications to list, and the list grows every day. Use a search engine such as Google to find what you're looking for. Following are sample criteria to employ as you wade through the possibilities:

- Is it free?
- Is it advertising supported?
- Is it designed for educational use? (Many are.)
- Are there privacy settings?
- What are the potential privacy issues?
- Is this app blocked by my school?
- Are there examples?

- Is there a tutorial?

- If it's for education, is there a teacher's guide?

- Has it been used and tested in K–12 classrooms?

- If students will use the tool, is it appropriate for their skill level?

- Does it meet the purposes of my instructional goals?

These are just a few examples of possible criteria for rating digital tools for the classroom. You will want to create your own list.

According to the New Media Consortium's Horizon Report (Johnson, 2009),

> Collaborative environments exist in myriad forms. They can be simple web-based tools for collaborative work, social networking platforms, community websites, classroom management systems, multiplayer gaming environments, or even virtual worlds. The common features that unite collaborative environments are that multiple people can work within them at once; that users can leave evidence of their thoughts, and reflections on the thoughts of others; and that they can support users in any location at any time. (p. 9)

Blogs

Short for *web logs*, blogs originated in the mid-1990s as personal, online journals where readers could subscribe and comment. Blogging instantly became popular as a remarkable vehicle for interactive exchanges of ideas. According to journalist Bryan Appleyard (2009) in his article *A Guide to the 100 Best Blogs, Part 1*, "The total number of blogs is thought to be approaching 200 million, 73 million of them in China."

Blogs encourage reader commentary. Generally, postings are listed chronologically by date, with the most current posting at the top of the list. The most successful blogs, the blogs that attract a following, are updated every day, or even more often. Readers are motivated to return by compelling, frequently updated content.

Blogs are used for all kinds of purposes by all kinds of people. Users can share thoughts, pictures, videos, podcasts, and links to other blogs as bloggers chronicle their lives, their thoughts, their ideas—more than we ever thought we wanted to know about what everyone else thinks about just about anything.

One way teachers might incorporate blogs into their STEM quest would be to have students follow blogs of professionals in their areas of interest. It is possible to find blogs written by just about any kind of STEM professional. Students would be able to ask questions via the commenting feature.

Another option is to set up a classroom blog and assign students to create posts on a rotating basis. Perhaps teachers could ask a STEM expert to read and comment on the posts on a regular basis. An authentic audience providing immediate feedback causes students to take blogging very seriously.

Microblogging

Twitter is a microblogging site, where users' posts, called *tweets*, are limited to 140 characters or less. Just like bloggers, users on Twitter attract a following. There are protocols for addressing another user in a tweet as well as "retweeting" a compelling tweet written by someone else. Perhaps most interestingly, Twitter boasts fairly robust search functionality, so it's possible to mine Twitter for commentary on any topic (some topics are given a hashtag—starting with the "#" symbol—for example, *#edtech*). Twitter also posts "trending topics" to let you know what topics are most commented on at any given moment.

Everyone from rock stars to school teachers seems to be tweeting these days. As frivolous as it sounds, there are already sound, innovative uses for tweets in the classroom.

- Student reflection on content
- Classroom extension
- Exchange of ideas and opinions/discussions
- Student/teacher collaboration
- Professional development/learning communities
- Promoting critical thinking skills

Tweets, or microblogs, create a sort of virtual collective stream of consciousness, but can also be harnessed for more specific purposes. Just as students might follow the blog of a STEM professional, they could also follow the Twitter account of a STEM professional. Maybe there's an astronaut who tweets, or a biologist helping to clean up an oil spill. The possibilities are endless. A class could start a Twitter account and tweet about the research they are doing.

Wikis

Blogging and microblogging are linear and are inefficient for interaction and input from large groups of people. The wiki, on the other hand, is nonlinear, with links to any number of user pages. Wikis allow potentially unlimited numbers of participants to create, modify, and collaborate. Like blogs, they function like a web page—they support the use of hypermedia—but the user doesn't need the expertise of a webmaster. The largest, and possibly most controversial, wiki is Wikipedia (www.wikipedia.org), the online encyclopedia that allows readers to edit and write information. It's used widely by students (and probably you, too) to grab quick information on almost any topic.

In the classroom, wikis can be used as a collaborative tool across the curriculum, for parent and administrator observation and input, for classroom newsletters, or to manage a large, collaborative project. For the Big Dig project (mentioned on page 72), a wiki would be a natural way to allow students to compile information over many months and edit collaboratively to achieve a final product.

Social Networking/Social Media

There is something almost primal about a social network. From the autographs we gathered in our high school yearbooks, or slambooks, to the many organizations we've joined over the years—personal or professional—as social creatures we are drawn to associate and share with peers. Social networking is the online version of a club or association of people who have come together for a common purpose. The purpose can be as broad as it is for Facebook—the desire to socialize—or it can be very specific—for example, a curriculum-based Ning for teachers.

> **SIXTY-TWO PERCENT** of educators have joined a social network and see high value for this technology in education.
>
> —*edWeb (2010)*

MySpace was one of the first social networking sites and at its peak reached over 80 million members. If it were a country, it would have been something like the 12th largest in the world. Facebook emerged on the tail of MySpace and is currently the most popular social network in the world, with more than 500 million members as of this writing. Facebook allows users to easily connect, converse, share, and comment.

**TOP 10
SOCIAL NETWORK SITES**
(by visitors per month)

Facebook	550,000,000
Twitter	95,800,000
Linkedin	50,000,000
MySpace	34,800,000
Ning	42,000,000
Tagged	30,000,000
Classmates	29,000,000
hi5	27,000,000
Myyearbook	12,000,000
Meetup	8,000,000

*Data from http://
socialnetworking.procon.org
February 2011*

The idea of social networking in the classroom still gets many people fired up. With any new application of this magnitude and with this kind of potential for abuse, it takes a while before teachers are ready to use it in the classroom as part of instruction, as a reasonable and essential pedagogical tool.

"We have to deal with it," says education writer Patrick J. McCloskey (2009) in an article in *Teacher Magazine*. He quotes Chris Lehmann, principal of the Science Leadership Academy in Philadelphia, "'Locking out the sites and tools of this new world our kids live in will render us irrelevant and useless when our students need us most … many of our students know how to reach a larger audience more quickly than any school district memo could ever hope to … our students need our help to make them understand how powerful that is. … We can build the 24/7/365 school if we embrace the technologies our students are already using'" (p. 27).

In the STEM arena, Facebook offers a wide variety of organizations to follow. Two examples are NASA and the Discovery Channel. Users navigate to the organization's page, click the "Like" button, and then begin receiving regular information from the organization in the form of posts, videos, and online resources.

Videoconferencing

Videoconferencing was one of the first digital tools used for distance learning and collaboration in the classroom. There is an up-front investment in equipment and infrastructure, but once the initial investment is paid for, videoconferencing is free. Room-sized videoconference equipment is the perfect tool to bring guest speakers and mentors into the classroom for live, face-to-face, and interactive meetings and events. More and more schools are using videoconferencing for virtual field trips and to provide classes from a distance that may not be offered in the home school. There are now hundreds of content providers offering virtual field trips for students to museums, science centers, university classrooms, and places of interest around the world.

The Center for Interactive Learning and Collaboration (CILC; www.cilc.org) has one of the largest directories of virtual field trip content providers. Other directories can be found at Two-Way Interactive Connections in Education (TWICE) (www.twice.cc) and Knowledge Network Explorer (www.kn.pacbell.com/wired/vidconf/ed1vidconf.html).

As Web 2.0 tools continue to proliferate, there are more desktop solutions for videoconferencing, but nothing beats the room-sized standard equipment for classes and ongoing collaborative programs for bringing partners into the classroom and for taking students on education excursions to places such as the Mote Marine Laboratory and Aquarium in Florida.

Skype

Anyone who can't afford to videoconference, can, for the price of a small eyeball camera, Skype for free. Skype is basically a phone call with video, and it's an effective way to add a collaborative dimension for students meeting with mentors or guest speakers. Perhaps you know a chemical engineer who is great with kids and a good speaker, but she's halfway across the country. No problem—Skype to the rescue!

TeacherTube

Most of us have heard of YouTube and have likely viewed at least one viral video on the site. I recently discovered TeacherTube while designing an online class for teachers. I was excited to find a safe haven for educational videos and a forum for education-related presentations. You don't have to be an expert to create video clips using your eyeball camera, a microphone, and Windows Movie Maker (or iMovie). TeacherTube hosts videos, just like YouTube, providing downloading and embedding capabilities for sharing the videos on other websites. TeacherTube provides privacy settings and user groups, and, of course, it's free.

There are countless STEM-related video clips available on TeacherTube. Teachers can use the robust search functionality to find exactly what they need. Or, they can have students create a video based on the students' research and upload it to TeacherTube.

Podcasts

Podcasting is a form of audio broadcasting on the web. I use the term *broad-casting* because in its strictest sense, a podcast is a digital, web-based broadcast using the radio-announcer style. Podcasts are used widely to create audio (and video) recordings in a digital format that can be listened to any time. Podcasts can be found across the Internet, but for starters you might try exploring iTunes and iTunes U. STEM content abounds there.

Tactics

Let's create an imaginary classroom in an imaginary school in today's real world. We are not professional curriculum designers, but together we can imagine ways to apply digital media tools in a middle school in the year 2010. It is late spring and the Gulf of Mexico oil spill has captured the attention of the world. People around the globe are participating in a critical international problem-solving effort—a teachable moment that many teachers have taken advantage of in their own classrooms.

Let me say first that this will be a simplistic, big-picture idea meant to inspire those who are not digital media experts, but rather beginners who might be looking for a place to start, looking for ways to use the digital tools and for project-based, hands-on ways to provide students with career awareness in the STEM fields using those tools.

Our imaginary school creates a schoolwide, cross-curricular, collaborative problem-solving effort using an issue such as the Gulf oil spill as the theme, with an additional focus on career exploration in environmental sciences. You could use any STEM-related theme, such as world health issues like obesity and contagious diseases, environmental issues like global warming, or a research project in which students might participate. We deploy a variety of digital media tools to facilitate our collaboration, research, networking, production, and final presentation of student work.

Teams are formed based on vocations and jobs within the following career tracks as listed with the U.S. Department of Labor: Environmental Biology, Environmental Engineering Technology, and Environmental Technology. As classroom teacher, or curriculum designer, you establish ways to apply the project design to existing content instructional strategies, goals, and objectives in all content areas.

The collaborative project could take place over the course of a term, semester, or an entire school year. Project participants make use of blogs, wikis, Nings (social networking), email, videoconferencing, podcasting, and digital story-telling. Web 2.0 applications are used as needed, and a technology support team including students is formed as part of the project. Some students subscribe to the blog of a biologist working on the cleanup, others subscribe to the Twitter feed of one of the mechanical engineers brainstorming ways to stop the flow of oil, and a leading ecologist is brought in via videoconference to address the students and answer questions.

The overall goals of our project include working together as teams to problem solve as part of the worldwide effort; to become familiar with specific science and engineering career tracks; and to provide an authentic setting in which to teach math, science, language arts, social studies, and art. Our desired outcomes might include:

- Learning about careers in environmental science, engineering, and technology
- Becoming proficient in digital technology skills
- Practicing and learning digital-age skills such as teamwork and collaboration
- Gaining leadership skills
- Learning how to pull together information from a wide range of sources
- Becoming proficient in networking skills through WebQuest activities
- Understanding and being able to present different perspectives
- Gaining proficiency in research skills and technical skills
- Understanding content and context
- Empowering students

Why do we list "empowering students" as a desired outcome? Because it can be said that young people are one of the largest groups of the disenfranchised. They have little say in what goes on in the world and sense this, though they may not be able to articulate the feeling. In this new culture of media collaboration, students are being offered opportunities to engage in civic debates, to participate in community life. Henry Jenkins states that "Empowerment comes from making meaningful decisions within a real civic context: we learn the skills of citizenship by becoming political actors and gradually coming to understand the choices we make in political terms" (2006, p. 10). Students are also likely to take inspiration from real people with whom they have developed relationships or whose roles they have observed and admired in a society they understand and where they feel a sense of belonging.

200 GOOD TEACHING IDEAS FOR SOCIAL NETWORKING

OnlineCollege.org posts 100 Ways You Should Be Using Facebook in Your Classroom: www.onlinecollege.org/ 2009/10/20/100-ways-you-should-be-using-facebook-in-your-classroom/

Emerging EdTech posts 100 Ways to Teach with Twitter: www.emergingedtech.com/ 2010/02/100-ways-to-teach-with-twitter/

Because our program could be viewed as an experimental learning environment, ongoing and pre- and postevaluations and assessments will be important because they have the power to:

- Provide critical information for teachers, administrators, school boards, funding sources, parents, and the community

- Provide a basis for changes/improvements and possible future funding

- Provide content for public relations materials and community outreach

- Empower future projects and continuation of the current project

To decide what tools to use, let's begin with our community space, a sort of project homeroom where we can meet and get to know each other, share information, and participate in ongoing dialogue. Consider Facebook for a moment. Many of you use it as a means to relax, stay in touch with friends, and share pictures with friends and relatives. Some of you think it's stupid—a waste of time. What if you could use the very same format to organize a schoolwide collaboration project?

Ning.com offers the bare bones from which you can develop a social networking, or social media, site that looks and feels much the same as Facebook, but the topic is the Gulf oil spill and career tracks in environmental science, engineering, and technology. Students and teachers become members; it is closed to the rest of the Internet. It becomes your own community and facilitates a schoolwide partnership—student-to-student, team-to-team, and classroom-to-classroom.

Science Centers and Online Science Learning Sites

Following are a handful of examples of the many online resources for educators and students sponsored by local and national professional science organizations and learning centers.

Cornell University, Department of Astronomy, Center for Radiophysics and Space Research, Education and Public Outreach
www.astro.cornell.edu/outreach/teachers

> Find them on Twitter or on their website where they welcome teachers by saying that they believe teachers are critical to the development of science literacy … for inspiring students to consider science, technology, and engineering careers. There are a lot of opportunities for educators and for students on this site, including grants, partnerships, and contests.

NASA for Educators
www.nasa.gov/audience/foreducators/

> NASA has created a rich online environment, filled with resources and inspiration, for both teachers and students, including a partnership with the Hubble Space Telescope Science Institute and the Amazing Space project. These programs, and programs offered through the Goddard Space Flight Center, provide curriculum content, cutting-edge visuals, and hands-on experiences that would never be available in a textbook-based classroom. They also provide professional development programs pairing educators with scientists and master educators.

SO MANY OF TODAY'S major technological breakthroughs were born from work done by NASA. Numerous modern innovations—from solar-power electricity generators, ultrasound scanners, and firefighters' breathing apparatus, to shock-absorbing athletic shoes and Velcro—are owed to the space program. NASA also has a place in education, offering great programs that can be solid alternatives to many of the pricey commercial curriculum supplements. NASA's website (www.nasa.gov) and the resources available there are in the public domain; the materials on the site are free to all. This puts some of the most recent discoveries in science and technology within reach of every educator (Werner, 2006).

National Climate Change and Wildlife Science Center
http://nccw.usgs.gov

At this center, sponsored by the U.S. Geological Survey, students and teachers interested in careers and related information in the field of climate change will find priorities for research needs and other critical information. Teachers interested in developing their own expertise in this area to share with the growing numbers of students interested in the topic could start here.

National Geographic Xpeditions
www.nationalgeographic.com/xpeditions/

This site, sponsored by *National Geographic Magazine*, outlines the U.S. National Geography Standards and offers a plethora of ideas, tools, and interactive adventures for teachers and students. Teachers can search the site's database to find "Xpeditions" related to specific curriculum. The site is organized by lesson plans, activities, standards, an atlas, and by geographic searches. Sign up for a free monthly newsletter.

Regional Science Center at Moorhead
www.mnstate.edu/regsci

A program of Minnesota State University Moorhead, this regional science center's website provides teacher training and opportunities in astronomy, biology, geology, and natural history. They work with school districts and partner with business and environmental organizations. Their list of projects and programs is inspirational.

Science and Discovery Center

www.sdcsciencecenter.org

> This is a regional science center in Central New York offering teacher workshops, student learning modules, and plenty of visual inspiration.

Science Learning Centres

www.sciencelearningcentres.org.uk

> Located in the United Kingdom, they have a primary focus on professional development for teachers in both K–12 and beyond, including teaching assistant training and training in science education for nonspecialists. Their website lists events, courses, resources, partnerships, and learning communities.

TERC: MSPNet

http://mspnet.org

> An online professional learning community, this site was created and is facilitated by the Center for School Reform at TERC; it is sponsored by the National Science Foundation. The online community is interactive and project based for the purpose of sharing an extensive knowledge base in the areas of math and science education and awareness. They have a library and all kinds of information resources for educators.

TUSD Regional Science Center

www.tusd1.org/contents/depart/science/index.asp

> Located in Tucson, Arizona, this regional science center's goal is to maintain a high-quality curriculum for K–12 science instruction. The site offers a calendar of professional development events. The organization works with Title II funding to support teachers.

Information Repositories

As the school works together in teams for problem-solving and exploration, students, teachers, and outside project partners post information and developments on a project wiki. Relevant links are posted on the wiki. Each team has its own wiki page, and assignments are also posted on the wiki.

Project Journals and Newsletter

Individuals or teams can use blogs as a way to reflect on their participation in the project—a kind of project journal. A project newsletter can be hosted on a wiki or a blog.

Project Communications

Communications tools such as interactive videoconferencing, instant messaging, and email are used to host guest speakers, mentors, and classroom partners from the professional community of environmental scientists. There are many possibilities for collaboration with a worldwide community of scientists and engineers.

Students create daily or weekly podcasts and post them on the project social network site (for example, Ning or similar, Facebook group, closed Facebook page). A podcast is much like a regular radio or television broadcast, so it is posted on a regularly scheduled day. Podcasts are created with MP3 tools and posted as a link on the community site.

This small sampling of ideas for project-based or place-based learning using digital tools is intended not to overwhelm, but rather to demonstrate some of the possibilities from a bird's-eye view. Clearly, ground rules for use of the technology need to be established at the start. If students are part of that process, they are more likely to hold each other accountable.

Culminating projects might include work that has been produced by students to share with the rest of the school and could consist of, for example, mash-ups of videos, writings, and digital storytelling. Projects and products could also be shared via YouTube or TeacherTube, on blogs, and on wikis. This is where teachers can let the students and the student teams help guide their own learning process, exercise ownership, and become engaged in authentic learning.

Why use so many different tools at once? Why integrate so many themes and cultural content? Why not just read a website that describes career tracks in STEM fields? In a recent report prepared for the MacArthur Foundation by digital media guru Henry Jenkins (2006) titled "Confronting the Challenges of Participatory Culture: Media Education for the 21st Century," he puts it this way:

> Rather than dealing with each technology in isolation, we would do better to take an ecological approach, thinking about the interrelationship among all of these different communication technologies, the cultural communities that grow up around them, and the activities they support. Media systems consist of communication technologies and the social, cultural, legal, political, and economic institutions, practices, and protocols that shape and surround them (Gitelman, 1999). The same task can be performed with a range of different technologies, and the same technology can be deployed toward a variety of different ends. Some tasks may be easier with some technologies than with others, and thus the introduction of a new technology may inspire certain uses. Yet, these activities become widespread only if the culture also supports them, if they fill recurring needs at a particular historical juncture. It matters what tools are available to a culture, but it matters more what that culture chooses to do with those tools. (p. 8)

Students will use the technology to research, share, and archive information; and by doing so, they will shape the culture of learning, learn by practice, and absorb content because it matters to them. Peers play a huge role in this. Students are learning how to participate in what many are now calling collective intelligence, where the community owns the work of the group and the individual contributes to the work of the group.

An important part of the group process is leadership. This can be modeled by teachers and professional role models, both in the school and in the professional world in which the students explore. Each project group may, through group process, select a project manager, providing an opportunity to model enterprise behavior and 21st-century skills.

An important lesson which should be part of any digital learning project is that there is a lack of reliable and credible information on the Internet. That doesn't mean not to use it; rather it means that the process should include fact-checking and information review. Students should learn the vetting process and how to evaluate information and sources.

Projects such as the one suggested here will also help shape students' under-standing of their own obligations and ethical boundaries while working on the Internet. Whether they create an individual blog or a community social media site, they will have to learn to follow the rules of copyright, the ethics of giving credit where credit is due and not taking credit for work that is not their own. Participating in authentic work is one way to learn those rules, especially if an informed classroom teacher is the project guide.

Take Off!

You're ready to get started. This section contains a few basic links from which to begin experimenting with blogs, wikis, and podcasts. Also listed are tools to help launch a classroom website, and an application that supports classroom-to-classroom and global learning partnerships.

The Basics

Curriki
www.curriki.org

> Curriki is an online community for sharing and creating open source K–12 curricula. The site currently has more than 40,000 registered users from countries all over the world.

Joomla
www.joomla.org/about-joomla.html

> Build your own website with Joomla, a free, open source content management system. You don't need to know HTML; the system manages the content for you.

OpenOffice
www.openoffice.org

> Get almost everything here you would pay for on the MS Office Suite, free. This productivity suite is sponsored primarily by Oracle; several corporations contribute to this open source project.

Collaboration/Communication Tools

Blogging Software Host Sites

Edublogs
http://edublogs.org

> This commercial blogging service is dedicated to education. The free version of Edublogs is supported by advertising; a paid version without the advertising is also available.

Elgg
http://elgg.org

> Elgg is actually an open source social networking engine with blogging capabilities. If you don't have your own web server, you'll need to subscribe to a hosting site.

WordPress
http://wordpress.org

> WordPress is a hugely popular open source blog host. Although it is not dedicated to education, the broad user base (more than 25 million users) and wealth of options and add-ons make it attractive.

Education-Related Blogs (a few favorites)

The Savvy Technologist
http://technosavvy.org

> Tim Wilson, a former classroom teacher now working as a chief technology officer in a public school in Minnesota, chats about technology integration from his perspective as a teacher. He tackles the subject of technology integration in an engaging manner—shoots from the hip. He started his musings several years ago with a focus on blogs and wikis, but the recent conversation about disruptive technology demonstrates the evolution to a more philosophic bent. I've listed this blog for the quality of the educational technology conversation, range of resources, and overall value for classroom teachers, both beginners and expert technologists and practitioners.

21Classes
www.21classes.com

> Use 21Classes to create a customized multiuser classroom blog portal. The service is free. Users like it because of the ease of customizing the blog sites and because it offers a number of features built off a centralized hub. Essentially, you can create a network of blogs under a veil of security, perfect for the classroom. It is a good tool to get students blogging. You could make a class home page, with a blog for each student. This could be used also as a career exploration tool, giving the classroom teacher a centralized location to monitor student activity. Comments have to be approved, slowing down comment spam.

Teacher Magazine Online, Teacher Blogs, Blogboard
www.edweek.org/tm/

> A publication of *Education Week*, *Teacher Magazine's* online version features a Blogboard listing top teacher blogs from around the country. Some of the best educator blogs cover topics such as "Road Diaries: Teacher of the Year," "Should Netbooks Be Required?" economics of education, and special education.

Podcast Directories

Education Podcast Network
http://epnweb.org

iTunes
www.itunes.com

Podcast.com
www.podcast.com

Podcast Directory
www.podcastdirectory.com

Podcasting News
www.podcastingnews.com

Social Media and Other Collaboration Tools

Facebook
www.facebook.com

Not just for kids—social networking is the collaborative and instructional digital tool of choice for innovative K–20 educators.

Glogster
http://www.glogster.com

Be sure to use the education version. Glogster has been dubbed an "interactive poster." It is essentially a website where students can work collaboratively or simply interact with each other.

Goodreads
www.goodreads.com

On this site, users share book lists and faves lists. The site also offers book discussion groups around specific areas of interest; a kind of online book club.

Google Docs
http://docs.google.com

This document-sharing tool for remote-located users also supports Microsoft's PowerPoint, Word, and Excel plus other spreadsheet-type documents.

LiveJournal
www.livejournal.com

This blog-hosting site contains topic-highlighted online journals on wide range of topics. Users can use it on their phones, send gifts, create books, and advertise. They describe themselves as an integrated hosting site.

Plurk
www.plurk.com

On this social media site, users create social journals—places to showcase life events without all the hoopla of the giants like Facebook. The site invites users to share (or Plurk) their "lifestreams."

Posterous
http://posterous.com

> Users can send media, via email, to this site, where the content is automatically posted. Also content can be autoposted to other social media sites.

TypePad
www.typepad.com

> TypePad is a social microblogging site that makes it easy to share photos.

VoiceThread
http://voicethread.com

> This is an online presentation tool. Users post slide shows consisting of various media with audio and text. It supports commentary using audio, text, and a doodling tool.

Microblogging

Twibes
http://twibes.com/edtech

Twitter Resources
www.iLearntechnology.com

> This edublog provides guidance for integrating tweets and other technologies.

Wiki Tools

MediaWiki
http://mediawiki.org

PBworks Wiki
http://pbwiki.com

PmWiki
http://pmwiki.com

Wikispaces
http://wikispaces.com

Instructional Tools

Engrade
www.engrade.com

> This classroom management tool features an assignment calendar, grade books, and a private messaging system that supports teacher/student/parent communications.

ePals
www.ePals.com

> This is a safe environment for students to collaborate from classroom to classroom, country to country. The ePals Global Learning Community serves over a half-million classrooms in 200 countries. ePals has supported some of the most compelling distance collaborations that have taken shape over the past decade. Even students who might be blocked from using blogs and wikis are able to access ePals. Their extreme safety features support email, blogging, translations, file sharing, and virus checking.

Moodle
http://moodle.org

> An open source course management system, or learning management system, Moodle is helping teachers manage project-based classrooms and share online courses. Although Moodle is free, it needs a server (district level) or web hoster and also requires staff training and product support. Moodle supports wikis and databases and is flexible enough to allow all kinds of creative applications. Think of it as an online classroom with face-to-face functions. Download Moodle for no charge.

WiZiQ
www.wiziq.com

> In this virtual classroom, users create online content and tests, reach out to remote content experts using digital communication tools, collaborate using PowerPoint, share audio and video, conduct live chats, and create social networks based on interest areas. Privacy and control options are available.

Organizational Tools

Blogged
www.blogged.com

> This searchable blog directory includes an education category. Find blogs on educational topics such as curriculum areas, political issues, instructional strategies, and the learning of languages.

Class Blogmeister
www.classblogmeister.com

> A quarter of a million featured educational blogs and bloggers appear on this blogging engine for educator.

Delicious
www.delicious.com

> Users of this social bookmarking site organize and share web pages and discover what others are using around topics of personal interest.

Diigo
www.diigo.com

> This social reading tool helps users organize and share bookmarks, and highlight or annotate portions of web pages.

Edtags
www.edtags.org

> This social bookmarking site was developed especially for educators. It is funded by Harvard University.

Educational Networking
www.educationalnetworking.com

> This wiki site hosts a list of social networks used in school environments.

Google blogs
http://blogsearch.google.com

> This is a search engine for blogs. Search terms can be turned into an RSS (really simple syndication) feed in Google Reader.

Netvibes
http://netvibes.com

> Netvibes is a personalized dashboard, or start page. Use it to organize online activity including mail, web storage, and news aggregation. You can use it for day-to-day tasks such as making to-do lists and organizing your mail. You can also use it to organize your blogging, podcasts, and widgets. Netvibes organizes your portal into tabs and bookmarks and can be personalized using themes and shared with a group. However, you should be aware that all shared content must be publicly available.

Technorati
www.technorati.com

> This blog search tool, or "reader" can be used as a kind of digital secretary to help keep you up-to-date with what you have found to be useful or important.

Twhirl
www.twhirl.org

> With this social software (microblogging) aggregator, users can organize social media such as Twitter, Friendfeed, Identi.ca, and Seesmic.

Other Resources

Kathy Schrock's Guide for Educators
http://school.discoveryeducation.com/schrockguide/sci-tech/scicom.html

CommonCraft Videos
www.commoncraft.com

> You may want to watch "Blogs in Plain English"—a video on this site that introduces blogging as a news source that brings like minds together. The video details how to construct a blog and how to facilitate conversation on a blog. $20.

Conclusion

THE IMPORTANCE OF PREPARING STUDENTS and developing curriculum content in the fields of science, technology, engineering, and mathematics (STEM) is now at the forefront of a national conversation in the United States, involving everyone from the president of the United States to local curriculum directors. Education leaders, politicians, corporate human resource experts, and education pundits have all called attention to the need for schools to produce leaders in this arena.

The goal, in part, is to prepare students for a world of work that requires knowledge workers in these fields who are as skilled and competent as those in other countries in the global economy. Even students who will one day work in the arts and the humanities will need strong foundations in STEM.

Everyone will need to be able to work in a collaborative rather than an autonomous environment. They will need to be critical thinkers, problem solvers, technicians, change agents, and lifelong learners. They will need fundamental judgment and social skills combined with skills in new technologies.

Although there are serious consequences for leaving students behind in a world that is rapidly changing and evolving, there are also numerous roadblocks to adopting, and adapting to, new tools and new strategies for teaching and learning: access, training, time, money, people. It's far too easy to blame teachers for not rushing to adopt these new tools and strategies, when the real problem is systemic.

Educators at all levels can use the tools and ideas put forth in this book, and in publications coming out on the Internet every day, to empower themselves to participate in the emerging society of independent learners. They can use these tools and ideas to make STEM a priority.

Evidence already shows that efforts to promote curricular subjects and career awareness in the STEM areas have met with success, particularly among girls and young women. Nevertheless, it is also true that even as students score higher on tests and seek more science-oriented college degrees, the number of students who actually want to pursue careers in STEM fields has remained static, even falling in some demographics.

Adding career awareness and interactive mentoring programs to the curriculum can be effective, especially when combined with efforts to create curriculum excitement. Media stereotypes and information gaps can be overcome by exposing students to real professionals working in exciting fields that students may not have known existed. Finding people to emulate is a powerful motivator for young people.

The key to success for classroom teachers and school administrators is to have open minds and be willing to explore the possibilities, often on their own time. The results could be new relationships between teachers and students who are learning and adapting across generations and across cultures.

The risks and barriers to opening our classrooms to all these opportunities are real, and they are significant. Yet the risks *can* be addressed; the tools for doing so are available and the rewards are too powerful to ignore. Building relationships with professionals who work in STEM fields will help prepare students by broadening their view of the possibilities, thus seeding the fertile soil of their passions and their imaginations. It's time to expand the horizon for every student and open our classrooms to the world.

National Educational Technology Standards

National Educational Technology Standards for Students (NETS•S)

All K–12 students should be prepared to meet the following standards and performance indicators.

1. Creativity and Innovation

Students demonstrate creative thinking, construct knowledge, and develop innovative products and processes using technology. Students:

    a. apply existing knowledge to generate new ideas, products, or processes

    b. create original works as a means of personal or group expression

    c. use models and simulations to explore complex systems and issues

    d. identify trends and forecast possibilities

2. Communication and Collaboration

Students use digital media and environments to communicate and work collaboratively, including at a distance, to support individual learning and contribute to the learning of others. Students:

    a. interact, collaborate, and publish with peers, experts, or others employing a variety of digital environments and media

    b. communicate information and ideas effectively to multiple audiences using a variety of media and formats

    c. develop cultural understanding and global awareness by engaging with learners of other cultures

    d. contribute to project teams to produce original works or solve problems

3. Research and Information Fluency

Students apply digital tools to gather, evaluate, and use information. Students:

a. plan strategies to guide inquiry

b. locate, organize, analyze, evaluate, synthesize, and ethically use information from a variety of sources and media

c. evaluate and select information sources and digital tools based on the appropriateness to specific tasks

d. process data and report results

4. Critical Thinking, Problem Solving, and Decision Making

Students use critical-thinking skills to plan and conduct research, manage projects, solve problems, and make informed decisions using appropriate digital tools and resources. Students:

a. identify and define authentic problems and significant questions for investigation

b. plan and manage activities to develop a solution or complete a project

c. collect and analyze data to identify solutions and make informed decisions

d. use multiple processes and diverse perspectives to explore alternative solutions

5. Digital Citizenship

Students understand human, cultural, and societal issues related to technology and practice legal and ethical behavior. Students:

a. advocate and practice the safe, legal, and responsible use of information and technology

b. exhibit a positive attitude toward using technology that supports collaboration, learning, and productivity

c. demonstrate personal responsibility for lifelong learning

d. exhibit leadership for digital citizenship

6. Technology Operations and Concepts

Students demonstrate a sound understanding of technology concepts, systems, and operations. Students:

a. understand and use technology systems

b. select and use applications effectively and productively

c. troubleshoot systems and applications

d. transfer current knowledge to the learning of new technologies

© 2007 International Society for Technology in Education (ISTE), www.iste.org. All rights reserved.

National Educational Technology Standards for Teachers (NETS•T)

All classroom teachers should be prepared to meet the following standards and performance indicators.

1. Facilitate and Inspire Student Learning and Creativity

Teachers use their knowledge of subject matter, teaching and learning, and technology to facilitate experiences that advance student learning, creativity, and innovation in both face-to-face and virtual environments. Teachers:

a. promote, support, and model creative and innovative thinking and inventiveness

b. engage students in exploring real-world issues and solving authentic problems using digital tools and resources

c. promote student reflection using collaborative tools to reveal and clarify students' conceptual understanding and thinking, planning, and creative processes

d. model collaborative knowledge construction by engaging in learning with students, colleagues, and others in face-to-face and virtual environments

2. Design and Develop Digital-Age Learning Experiences and Assessments

Teachers design, develop, and evaluate authentic learning experiences and assessments incorporating contemporary tools and resources to maximize content learning in context and to develop the knowledge, skills, and attitudes identified in the NETS•S. Teachers:

a. design or adapt relevant learning experiences that incorporate digital tools and resources to promote student learning and creativity

b. develop technology-enriched learning environments that enable all students to pursue their individual curiosities and become active participants in setting their own educational goals, managing their own learning, and assessing their own progress

    c. customize and personalize learning activities to address students' diverse learning styles, working strategies, and abilities using digital tools and resources

    d. provide students with multiple and varied formative and summative assessments aligned with content and technology standards and use resulting data to inform learning and teaching

3. Model Digital-Age Work and Learning

Teachers exhibit knowledge, skills, and work processes representative of an innovative professional in a global and digital society. Teachers:

    a. demonstrate fluency in technology systems and the transfer of current knowledge to new technologies and situations

    b. collaborate with students, peers, parents, and community members using digital tools and resources to support student success and innovation

    c. communicate relevant information and ideas effectively to students, parents, and peers using a variety of digital-age media and formats

    d. model and facilitate effective use of current and emerging digital tools to locate, analyze, evaluate, and use information resources to support research and learning

4. Promote and Model Digital Citizenship and Responsibility

Teachers understand local and global societal issues and responsibilities in an evolving digital culture and exhibit legal and ethical behavior in their professional practices. Teachers:

    a. advocate, model, and teach safe, legal, and ethical use of digital information and technology, including respect for copyright, intellectual property, and the appropriate documentation of sources

    b. address the diverse needs of all learners by using learner-centered strategies and providing equitable access to appropriate digital tools and resources

    c. promote and model digital etiquette and responsible social interactions related to the use of technology and information

   d. develop and model cultural understanding and global awareness by engaging with colleagues and students of other cultures using digital-age communication and collaboration tools

5. Engage in Professional Growth and Leadership

Teachers continuously improve their professional practice, model lifelong learning, and exhibit leadership in their school and professional community by promoting and demonstrating the effective use of digital tools and resources. Teachers:

   a. participate in local and global learning communities to explore creative applications of technology to improve student learning

   b. exhibit leadership by demonstrating a vision of technology infusion, participating in shared decision making and community building, and developing the leadership and technology skills of others

   c. evaluate and reflect on current research and professional practice on a regular basis to make effective use of existing and emerging digital tools and resources in support of student learning

   d. contribute to the effectiveness, vitality, and self-renewal of the teaching profession and of their school and community

National Educational Technology Standards for Administrators (NETS•A)

All school administrators should be prepared to meet the following standards and performance indicators.

1. Visionary Leadership

Educational Administrators inspire and lead development and implementation of a shared vision for comprehensive integration of technology to promote excellence and support transformation throughout the organization. Educational Administrators:

   a. inspire and facilitate among all stakeholders a shared vision of purposeful change that maximizes use of digital-age resources to meet and exceed learning goals, support effective instructional practice, and maximize performance of district and school leaders

   b. engage in an ongoing process to develop, implement, and communicate technology-infused strategic plans aligned with a shared vision

   c. advocate on local, state, and national levels for policies, programs, and funding to support implementation of a technology-infused vision and strategic plan

2. Digital-Age Learning Culture

Educational Administrators create, promote, and sustain a dynamic, digital-age learning culture that provides a rigorous, relevant, and engaging education for all students. Educational Administrators:

   a. ensure instructional innovation focused on continuous improvement of digital-age learning

   b. model and promote the frequent and effective use of technology for learning

   c. provide learner-centered environments equipped with technology and learning resources to meet the individual, diverse needs of all learners

   d. ensure effective practice in the study of technology and its infusion across the curriculum

e. promote and participate in local, national, and global learning communities that stimulate innovation, creativity, and digital-age collaboration

3. Excellence in Professional Practice

Educational Administrators promote an environment of professional learning and innovation that empowers educators to enhance student learning through the infusion of contemporary technologies and digital resources. Educational Administrators:

a. allocate time, resources, and access to ensure ongoing professional growth in technology fluency and integration

b. facilitate and participate in learning communities that stimulate, nurture, and support administrators, faculty, and staff in the study and use of technology

c. promote and model effective communication and collaboration among stakeholders using digital-age tools

d. stay abreast of educational research and emerging trends regarding effective use of technology and encourage evaluation of new technologies for their potential to improve student learning

4. Systemic Improvement

Educational Administrators provide digital-age leadership and management to continuously improve the organization through the effective use of information and technology resources. Educational Administrators:

a. lead purposeful change to maximize the achievement of learning goals through the appropriate use of technology and media-rich resources

b. collaborate to establish metrics, collect and analyze data, interpret results, and share findings to improve staff performance and student learning

c. recruit and retain highly competent personnel who use technology creatively and proficiently to advance academic and operational goals

d. establish and leverage strategic partnerships to support systemic improvement

e. establish and maintain a robust infrastructure for technology including integrated, interoperable technology systems to support management, operations, teaching, and learning

5. Digital Citizenship

Educational Administrators model and facilitate understanding of social, ethical, and legal issues and responsibilities related to an evolving digital culture. Educational Administrators:

a. ensure equitable access to appropriate digital tools and resources to meet the needs of all learners

b. promote, model, and establish policies for safe, legal, and ethical use of digital information and technology

c. promote and model responsible social interactions related to the use of technology and information

d. model and facilitate the development of a shared cultural understanding and involvement in global issues through the use of contemporary communication and collaboration tools

References

Appleyard, B. (2009, February 15). A guide to the 100 best blogs, part 1. *The Sunday Times* [Online]. Available from http://technology.timesonline.co.uk/tol/news/tech_and_web/the_web/article5725644.ece

Barrington, L., & Mitchell, C. (2008). *Investing in the future—the importance of cross-sector partnerships in improving workforce readiness* (Executive Action Report # A-0258-08-EA). New York, NY: The Conference Board.

Business Wire. (2009, October 20). *Massachusetts coalition launches innovative program to boost student interest in math, science careers.* Available from http://findarticles.com/p/articles/mi_m0EIN/is_20091020/ai_n39304199/

Edutopia (Producer). (2010). *Digital media empower youth.* [Video]. Available from www.edutopia.org/digital-generation-youth-network-video

edWeb (2010). School principals and social networking in education: practices, policies, and realities in 2010. Available from www.guide2digitallearning.com/professional_development/school_principals_and_social_networking_0

Gitelman, L. (1999). Scripts, grooves, and writing machines: Representing technology in the Edison Era. Stanford, CA: Stanford University Press.

Government Technology. (2008, February 6). *Classrooms for the future grant program arrives in Harrisburg, PA.* Available from www.govtech.com/e-government/Classrooms-for-the-Future-Grant-Program.html

Institute for a Competitive Workforce, U.S. Chamber of Commerce. (2008). *The skills imperative: How career and technical education can solve the U.S. talent shortage.* Washington, DC: Author.

Jenkins, H. (2006). *Confronting the challenges of participatory culture: Media education for the 21st century.* The MacArthur Foundation. Available from http://newmedialiteracies.org/files/working/NMLWhitePaper.pdf

Johnson, L., Levine, A., Smith, R., & Smythe, T. (2009). *The 2009 Horizon report: K–12 edition.* Austin, TX: The New Media Consortium.

Matthews, C. (2007). *Science, engineering, and mathematics education: Status and issues.* CRS Report for Congress. Available at http://digitalcommons.unl.edu/crsdocs/3/

McCloskey, P. (2009). The blogvangelist. *Teacher Magazine, 18*(2), 22–24, 27–29.

Michigan Department of Education (n.d.). http://www.michigan.gov/mde/0,4615,7-140-38924_52164-220902--,00.html

National Commission on Excellence in Education. (1983). A nation at risk: The imperative for educational reform. *Elementary School Journal 84*(2) pp. 112-130.

Pain, E., & Carpenter, S. (2009, November 27). Careers in climate change research: Feature index. *Science Career Magazine.* Retrieved from http://sciencecareers.sciencemag.org/career_magazine/previous_issues/articles/2009_11_27/caredit.a0900145

Prabhu, M. T. (2010, January 6). National STEM program increases reach: President Obama honors outstanding math and science educators as new partnerships emerge in the push to improve STEM education. eSchool News. Available from www.eschoolnews.com/2010/01/06/educate-to-innovate-program-increases-reach/2/

Survey: 77% of teens interested in STEM career. (2010, January 28). *Tech & Learning.* Available at www.techlearning.com/article/27336

Thornburg, D. D. (1994). *Education in the communication age.* San Carlos, CA: Starsong Publications.

Time Warner Cable (2009, November 23). Time Warner Cable to connect a million minds. [Press Release]. Available from www.timewarnercable.com/Nebraska/about/inthenewsdetails.ashx?PRID=2736&MarketID=49

Werner, C. (2006). The answer is in the stars. *T.H.E. Journal, 23*(14), 4.

Wisconsin Department of Public Instruction (2006). *State superintendent's high school task force report.* Available from dpi.wi.gov/sprntdnt/pdf/hstask_report.pdf

Index